FEMI OLAJIGA

Foreword by ARIE VAN BENNEKUM

(Co-author of the Agile Manifesto)

LEAN AGILE MARKETING
How to Become Agile and Deliver Marketing Success

Published in the United Kingdom in 2017 by CX Conversion Ltd.

11 The Approach, Northampton, Northamptonshire, NN5 5FF

Content © Femi Olajiga, 2017

Foreword © Arie van Bennekum, 2017

Case Study One © Peter Eggleston, 2017

Case Study Two © Julee Bellomo, 2017

Case Study Three © Emma Sharrock, 2017

Case Study Four © Michael McKinnon, 2017

Case Study Five © Mia Kolmodin, 2017

Case Study Six © Sam Zawadi, 2017

Case Study Seven © Monica Georgieff, 2017

Case Study Eight © Peter Billante, 2017

Case Study Nine © Marina Simonova, 2017

Illustrations and Graphic Design © Antonija Saric, 2017

British Library Cataloguing-in-Publication Data

A CIP record for this book is available from the British Library

ISBN Print: 978-0-9957465-0-3

ISBN eBook: 978-0-9957465-1-0

Printed and bound by Amazon.com, Inc.

Typeset by Antonija Saric

Thank you to the thousands of agile leaders around the world for creating the agile values and principles that marketing teams can learn from – to sharpen their thinking and shift their mindset.

Thank you to my family: Olori, Bubu, my parents, siblings, Nonne, my relatives and Bestie & Co. And in remembrance of the special people we lost too soon, I will never forget you: Yeye Akogun and Nonno.

Contents

Case Studies

Foreword

by Arie van Bennekum

Back in 1994 it was for me a very conscious choice: 'this is how I don't want to work anymore'. Yes, of course, my background is in IT and at that time I was working as a technical designer, but that does not mean that my focus was limited to the professional domain of IT. When I took my first steps in 1994 in what we call Agile today, it was always as a project manager responsible for a full delivery solution to development projects. Everything was in there: legal, ops, dev, marketing, communication – there were no exceptions. It was the whole package, from start to finish, from scratch to operational use, including adapting business processes, training people, connecting marketing campaigns, and implementing operational teams.

The question always was – and still remains – how can we best employ this efficient and effective way of working as one team, sometimes containing as many as 40 people? I remember many evenings trying to figure out how to do it and then the next day putting it into practice. This is for me what real Agile has always been and always will be: experimenting, reusing best practice, and therefore as an individual, being open to learn from others' best practice, and learning (sometimes hard) lessons. And a lesson learned means not stepping back into old routines when things go wrong. It means looking at how we can make it work within this efficient and effective way of working. The professional domain of marketing is already familiar with the Agile concept, at least in the region of the world where I spend most of my time. We have early adopters and innovators across the world and in every profession. In the marketing world there have been some very interesting publications already. Here is another one. With Femi Olajiga taking the lead, he has brought together his own practice, ideas and relevant case studies from Agile marketing leaders around the world. Read the book and try out what works well for you. Adopt the proper attitude towards this hard labour of achieving your goal. Be guided by the Agile Manifesto, experiment with Femi's suggestions, and reap your benefits. Enjoy!

Introduction

In order to market effectively, it is vital to consider an iterative approach to planning which is regularly informed by customer experience insights. As such, this is the first book on agile marketing that has been based on the collective experience of agile marketing professionals, reflecting their varied approaches to adopting agile within marketing and sales teams. It provides an in-depth insight into how agile marketing professionals are implementing agile methodologies within their campaign planning and execution.

Chapter one introduces the core concepts of agile and discusses agile values and principles in the context of marketing teams - without recourse to any IT jargon. The chapter also outlines the thoughts of agile marketing thought leaders from around the world on the essential elements of agile marketing. Chapter two explores the role of mindset in the adoption and successful adaptation of agile for marketing purposes, with an emphasis on emotional intelligence, personality types and the role of personal development in the successful implementation of agile within teams. Chapter three emphasises the role of customer insights in shaping an organization's marketing strategy. Particular attention is paid to how marketing teams can improve customer experience through detailed customer research, customer profiles, customer segments and customer journey maps. This chapter also highlights the role of customer journey mapping in aligning the various silos within the organization in order to create a seamless customer experience. Chapter four then delves into the practicalities of implementing agile within a marketing context, highlighting the role of a detailed situation analysis and identifying challenges that teams are likely to face in this process, as well as benefits they are likely to experience. Chapter five is the concluding chapter which comprises a series of practical case studies contributed by practitioners within the industry. These agile marketing thought leaders share their individual stories about how they implemented agile marketing within their teams. Each case study provides a different angle on agile implementation within different organizational contexts, from IT (software development) to marketing, sales, human resources and project management functions.

This step-by-step guide of adopting agile into marketing is essential reading for anyone who wishes to remain relevant and competitive in today's volatile market.

Case study contributor profiles

Arie van Bennekum: Co-author, Agile Manifesto

Arie van Bennekum is an international Agile transformation expert and one of the authors of the 2001 Agile Manifesto. He is an expert in the area of Agile project management, team facilitation, Agile techniques and user involvement. For him, Agile is a universal interaction concept based on ten interaction rituals that can be applied in every professional domain.

Arie has successfully implemented Agile in medium-sized, as well as large international organizations operating in a range of industries, including retail, technology, energy supply, finance, and others. He has developed the Integrated AgileTM Transformation Model (IATM) for full corporate transformations, connecting all entities in an organization working with Agile, from HR to marketing, and from sales to IT.

Peter Billante: Vice President Product Management | Marketing at Autodesk

Peter Billante has over 20 years of experience within the software industry and currently leads marketing for Autodesk's BIM 360, a platform of mobile and cloud-based applications purpose-built for the construction industry. Pete joined Autodesk in 2012, through the acquisition of Vela Systems, where he was VP of Product Management. Pete also led product management at OAT Systems, an RFID software company acquired by Checkpoint Systems, and Frictionless Commerce, which was acquired by SAP. Prior to this, he held positions at SAP America and Procter & Gamble. Pete graduated from Vanderbilt University with a degree in Electrical Engineering and Computer Science, and holds an MBA from MIT's Sloan School of Management.

Brian Raboin: Vice President of Customer Experience at Booker Software

Brian Raboin has been working in the world of technology and customer experience since 2001 when he was the fifth employee at HostMySite.com/Hosting.com. Brian was the Vice President of Operations with HostMySite when the company acquired Hosting.com in 2008.

During his career, Brian held multiple titles with various responsibilities, including Vice President of Product, Vice President of Customer Experience, Chief Customer Officer and Chief Strategy Officer. Brian became a thought leader in the world of Customer Experience and was the keynote speaker at IQPC's Call Center week in 2013, the Customer Keynote at Oracle's Service Cloud Sales Kickoff FY2014, an invited speaker at OracleWorld 2014, and he continues to be an active contributor to the world of Customer Experience and the practical application of Customer Experience Journey Mapping.

Brian has a Bachelor's degree in history and various other technical and business program certifications from the University of Delaware. Additionally, he is a certified Scrum Master, certified Net Promoter Associate, Pragmatic Marketing Product Management Certified and ITIL Foundation Certified. He now resides in Scottsdale, Arizona with his wife and two children. He is currently at Booker Software, the creators of a SaaS-based platform that automates the business operations of the health, wellness and beauty industries, as their Vice President of Customer Experience.

Sean Zinsmeister: Vice President of Product Marketing at Infer.com

Sean Zinsmeister is the VP of Product Marketing at Infer, where he's responsible for crafting the positioning, messaging and overall go-to-market strategy for Infer's next-generation predictive sales and marketing platform. Once a satisfied Infer customer himself, Sean joined Infer from Nitro, where he developed and led an award-winning global marketing operations team.

As a thought-leader and accomplished sales and marketing technologist, Sean's work has been featured by Salesforce, Marketo, Hubspot, Microsoft, Business 2 Community, VentureBeat, and MarketingLand, among others. In addition to these public works, he is also founder and co-host of the Stack & Flow podcast, one of the top sales and marketing technology broadcasts in the industry. Sean holds advanced degrees from Suffolk Sawyer School of Business and Northeastern, respectively in strategic marketing and project management.

Sam Zawadi: Lean Agile Coach

Sam is a Lean-Agile coach at Projectiv, helping teams and organisations to become more agile. Sam's most recent client engagements have been working with Freeview to deliver and launch the UK-wide Freeview Play TV service, and working with Microsoft on the worldwide launch of Xbox One and associated core apps. Currently, Sam is helping Aimia Inc. use scaled agile approaches to transform and deliver large product development initiatives using lean-agile approaches, and is also creating a business agility initiative aimed at non IT teams such as HR, which is being adopted throughout the organisation.

Sam is also the founder of DPML (http://www.meetup.com/london-digital-project-managers/), an education and learning group that runs Agile focused events for project, programme and delivery management professionals. He is currently collaborating with leading agile professionals in the industry to help make enterprise agility more widely understood and practiced across different business.

Please visit https://www.meetup.com/agileDPML/ to get in touch with Sam or to learn more.

Michael McKinnon: Global Marketing Operations at Avaya.com

Michael McKinnon has 15 years of experience in B2B marketing in roles spanning from demand generation to marketing operations. He is currently in the Global Marketing Operations organization at Avaya where he oversees their global lead flow, pipeline metrics and lead management. Implementing an agile methodology with a global team, Mike was able to build a global lead-scoring model, lead nurture tracks across all BUs and implement the Sirius Decisions waterfall methodology for lead tracking and revenue attribution within a year. In 2011, in his previous position at ReadyTalk, Mike implemented an agile methodology within his team. Moving through different process versions, software models and variants, Mike was able to build team unity, break down company silos and eliminate project creep. Mike is a sought-after speaker for industry events. He is a repeat speaker at Oracle's Modern Marketing Experience and has also spoken at SXSW. He has written numerous articles on the role of automation in an organization and on best practices.

Monica Georgieff: Head of Marketing at Kanbanize

Monica Georgieff is the Head of Marketing at Kanbanize, a European SaaS company, where she helps new-generation companies apply the Lean Kanban method to their teams' processes in order to develop software 3X faster, beat their competition and exceed the expectations of their own customers. She's a creative–techie hybrid with a background in the Canadian publishing industry and a literary education. She believes the future of marketing is in thinking Lean and that data is in the details.

Kanbanize is an innovative and growing Lean platform bringing visualization, automation and efficiency to the field of product development through its namesake web-based software. The software's arsenal of features includes a flexible automations engine, powerful analytics module, as well as the ability to create a breakdown and hierarchy of your tasks using links between cards. Kanbanize helps teams, ranging from emerging organizations to Fortune 500 enterprises, to succeed by cultivating a consistent workflow and continually improving the rate at which they generate value.

Dave Dame: Agile Leader at Scotiabank

Dave Dame is a leadership coach, enterprise agile leader and trainer with over 20 years of management experience and a reputation for facilitating the practical implementation of agile practices in large organizations. Dave has successfully led complex agile transformations that include scaling specialized resources, implementing regulatory compliance, legacy products, and scaling agile practices across large enterprises such as OpenText, PTC, and MCAP. He is well seasoned in coaching executives, managers, and non-technical departments, as well as building up high-performing teams of Scrum Masters, Product Owners and Agile Coaches. He brings his expertise to organizations through teaching and mentoring as well as serving as an agile coach and facilitator. Dave joined Scotiabank in July 2016 as Agile Leader, Digital Factory. In this role he is focused on helping employees and teams become empowered to 'be the change' that will bring industry-leading products to market through agile practices.

David Grabel: Enterprise Agile Coach at Vistaprint

Currently bringing agile to the entire business unit at Vistaprint, David Grabel is a passionate enterprise agile coach. He coached the internal advertising agency and the email marketing channel at Vistaprint, bringing Agile to marketing. He has introduced agile to organizations of different sizes, from single-team start-ups to large organizations with over 500 teams. His previous clients include PayPal, Bose, and Trizetto. He helped develop a process for integrating Lean UX design with Scrum delivery teams that was rolled out to 15 Lean UX teams supporting over 100 delivery teams around the world.

He has presented at several Agile events including Agile 2015, Agile 2016, Mile High Agile, and Lean Kanban North America, the first annual Business Agility conference. David is a past president of Agile New England. Previously, he was Vice President of Engineering at Monetrics a startup that was acquired by JM Family Enterprises. Other previous senior management positions include Vice President of Product Technology at Thomson Gale and Vice President of Development at Politzer & Haney.

Peter Eggleston: Senior Global Product Marketing Manager at GE Healthcare

Peter Eggleston has over 25 years of experience in high tech start-ups and early stage companies bringing SaaS products to market, some leading to successful exits to companies such as Google and Hewlett Packard. He is currently Senior Global Product Marketing Manager for GE Healthcare and has an extensive frontline and leadership experience in product design, marketing and business development. His previous roles include SVP of U.S. Commercial Products at Aptus Health, CMO of SBR Health, Founder and CEO of AdME, Inc., VP of Sales & Marketing for Sonic Network, Inc., and Senior Director of Business Development at Millivision, LLC. Pete has served as an adjunct faculty member at Northeastern University and the Rochester Institute of Technology, has authored over 40 papers, articles, and talks at industry conferences, anchored columns in two industry magazines, writes a blog on agile marketing and business development principles and has served on the advisory boards of several start-up companies and organizations throughout the New England area.

Emma (Bryce) Sharrock: Author of The Agile Project Manager

Emma (Bryce) Sharrock is passionate about all things that involve change and people. Her career began as an officer in the Royal Australian Navy, and she has worked as a project and change manager since 1999. Emma founded a coaching business in 2011, and since then has been working on 'converging' her passions for projects, change and human behaviour.

Emma published her first book, The Agile Project Manager, in November 2015 with the goal of providing simple tools and techniques to enable project professionals to achieve great outcomes with Agile. Since then, she has worked with people, teams and organizations to facilitate their Agile transformations through coaching, consulting and training.

Marina Simonova: Agile transformation coach

Marina Simonova is a certified coach and a professional facilitator with experience of agile transformation in over 60 sales and marketing teams across Europe. Marina is the founder of Agile Space company and also creates and designs training for non-IT Scrum Masters. Marina has over 10 years of experience in Russia's top financial companies and is a regular speaker at Agile Outside IT events.

Julee Bellomo: Agile Consultant

Julee Bellomo is an experienced Agile practitioner based in Tampa, Florida. As a senior consultant within Agile Thoughts Agile Practice, she leads Agile transformations, consulting, coaching, and training efforts. Julee enjoys applying Agile techniques to teams outside software development, including BI, marketing, visual/media teams, and project management offices. She brings a specialty in ideation, change management, product ownership and large-group facilitation with a focus on lean start-up thinking and innovation games. Julee is active in both the Agile and project management communities; she is the founder of the Tampa Bay Product Owner group and actively participates in community Agile and technology. Previously, Julee has been part of the leadership and PMO teams at AARP, Deltek, and Marriott, amongst others. As a principal at Opal Consulting LLC since 2014, Julee is a public trainer, speaker and blogger. You can read her thoughts at www.theagilecorner.com or on LinkedIn Pulse.

Richard Sheridan, CEO Menlo Innovations and Author of best selling book, Joy, Inc

Richard Sheridan is the CEO of Menlo Innovations, one of the few companies in the world that has implemented agility across the entire organization. With a steadfast commitment to simplifying the process of creating cutting-edge technological solutions, Rich focused his career on creating a workplace filled with camaraderie, human energy, creativity and productivity, following an inspirational visit to the Edison Menlo Park New Jersey Lab.

In 2001, together with James Goebel, Rich co-founded a company whose purpose is to "end human suffering in the world as it relates to technology" by returning joy to one of the most unique endeavors mankind has ever undertaken: the invention of software. Their unique approach to custom software design, High-tech Anthropology®, has since produced custom software that delights users and makes software design a joy to experience. Menlonians regularly share their knowledge and experience with thousands of professionals from around the world interested in studying 'The Menlo Way'. His book, Joy, Inc. - How We Built a Workplace People Love was published in 2013 by Penguin Random House and now has Rich traveling the world speaking about joy, creativity, and human energy in the workplace.

Chapter 1: Introduction to agile

Background

In the past couple of decades, agile has been implemented in a range of settings, from individual teams to entire organizations, as well as within specific business functions, such as marketing, legal, human resources, finance, project management and others. In fact, agile is becoming more and more relevant in a range of industries, most notably those that are open and welcoming to entrepreneurial start-ups that are able to quickly eat into current players' market shares. In writing this book, I spent a lot of time speaking with Arie van Bennekum (co-author of *Agile Manifesto* of 2001), who has been a practitioner of and advocate for agile in non-IT environments since as far back as 1996. For him, agile is much more than a software development framework; he sees it as an interaction process between individuals and teams that can have a seismic impact on team effectiveness and, ultimately, business revenue. Although technology is its powerful enabler, both Arie and I believe that the true power of agile is in the rituals between different stakeholders within and across marketing teams: the moment teams embrace the core principles of agile and its core ways of working (rituals), the implementation of agile becomes possible at every level of an organization. Think about it: some of the most agile entities in the world are the teams in a hospital operating theatre, or the special forces teams behind enemy lines. These teams are highly trained, disciplined, share common objectives and work in a highly co-ordinated way. Nevertheless, there are instances where unforeseen situations will arise. And how do these teams respond? They survive because they have a strong agreement and understanding as to how they function as a team. The U.S. Army website describes the special forces team structure as follows: '*Special Forces Teams are generally organized into small, versatile groups, called Operational Detachment Alphas*'. Each team contains 12 members with '*his own speciality: Weapons Sergeants, Communication Sergeants, Medical Sergeants and Engineering Sergeants*' and '*A Commander, Assistant and Non-Commissioned Officer in charge*'. The agility of these teams is based on trust: every member of the team is able to trust and count on the man to their left, right, front and back. They each understand that every member's contribution is essential to the overall success of the team. A typical Green Beret team comprises individuals with specialist skills and two leaders within the team, the commanding officer and the second-in-command (which is a similar set-up to that of the CMO and team leader in a marketing context). Apart from the two leadership positions, there are five pairs of specialist positions for intelligence, communication, operations, medical, engineering and weapons. This team is able to function perfectly as an independent unit – which is what makes them the perfect agile team.

Special Forces selection

Special forces teams are chosen after completing an intensive six-month pre-selection process. They are then subjected to real-life tasks under extreme conditions that are designed to break them physically and mentally, with the main aim of playing on their self-doubts, fears and endurance limits to evaluate how well they would perform under pressure. Would they be able to work as individuals and as part of a team? Would each individual within the special forces team be able to cope with their personal struggles under extreme physical conditions in order to complete the team mission? Would they possess the necessary physical and mental stamina, combined with the ability to remain calm in dangerous situations? Members of these teams are expected to conquer situations that push through their physical pain thresholds and overcome their mental barriers that make other people quit when faced with the same situation.

NATO defines special operations as 'military activities conducted by specially designated, organized, trained, and equipped forces, manned with selected personnel, using unconventional tactics, techniques, and modes of employment'.

Although they will never be faced with true life or death situations like the special forces teams, marketing teams play an important role in the survival of a business, so making agility a priority makes sense from a purely financial perspective. Arie believes that embedding lean and Kanban principles into marketing is the best way for marketing teams to follow in the footsteps of the special forces teams. Some companies are way ahead in this game: agile organizations such as Netflix, Spotify, Menlo Innovations, and ING Bank routinely refer to their teams as 'squads'. As is the case with special forces, agile marketing teams contain individuals with different areas of expertise and skills' backgrounds, with an emphasis on high levels of emotional intelligence and a whole range of soft skills. Both are groups of autonomous and self-organizing individuals, responsible for the end-to-end planning and execution of marketing campaigns, lead by strong team leaders (Commanding Officer vs Scrum Master/Product Owner). Both teams need to be highly trained and responsive to the changes in their environment, and both have one main objective: to deliver bottom line value to the organization they are a part of. In the end, both are living, breathing, learning, iterative organizations, and as such are fertile ground for embedding agility.

What is agile marketing?

Let's start this section with a generic and somewhat simplified overview of marketing. Put simply, marketing is communication from one person (or entity) to the other with the sole aim of selling a product or service. The process starts with research and an understanding of the value that each person is interested in exchanging with the other. Companies create products and customers use these products in exchange for financial payment. A similar (although not exactly the same!) process applies to a marriage or a long-term relationship between two people. A relationship starts with communication between two people with the initial aim of learning more about each other's likes and dislikes. They go on dates, meet each other's friends and, if things get serious, it can eventually lead to marriage. Obviously, marriage does not guarantee that the relationship will last forever but the foundation of trust, respect, passion, communication and compatibility will determine how long the relationship lasts. This is exactly what marketing is all about: companies start by communicating with customers to explain the value inherent in their product or service in order to convince the customer to make their first purchase: this constitutes the first phase. The second phase of marketing is establishing a relationship with the customer to encourage repeat purchases and the third phase is trying to build the customer's trust with the aim of converting him or her into a brand advocate (or ambassador), thus establishing a long-term relationship with the organization. So, I guess it would fair to say that anyone who has ever been in any form of relationship with another person has experienced first-hand the fundamental process of marketing. From a business perspective, the marketing process is further enhanced with the range of technology platforms and tools now available to marketing teams, but the fundamental concept is always the same no matter which tool or channel companies use to engage with their customers. The marketing process can be divided into the following phases:

» Acquiring customers;

» Engaging with customers;

» Convincing customers to buy;

» Building long-term trust with customers.

Agile marketing teams are structured like sports teams. Every team has a coach that helps individuals within the team to develop. These coaches do not tell their teams how to do their jobs, but work together with them to develop a winning strategy, all the while empowering

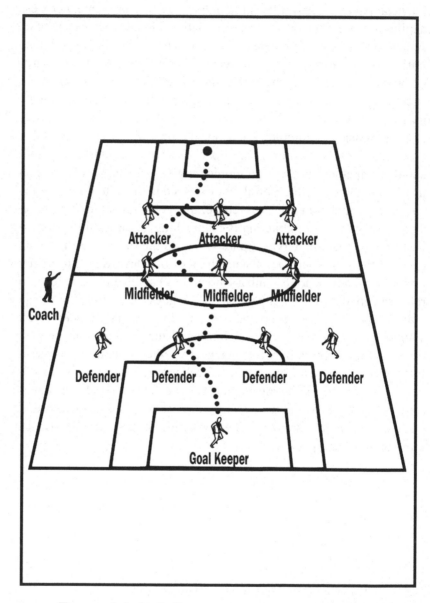

Teamwork in football

the team to make decisions. Like in football, a group of individuals are responsible for protecting the team from conceding goals from the opposing side. This is the same way individuals in agile marketing teams are responsible for implementing customer retention strategy. Football teams have individuals responsible for scoring goals in their opponent's net, while in marketing teams individuals are responsible for customer acquisition. Football teams make sure they score more goals while conceding less from the opposition, whereasnon-agile marketing teams seem to do the exact opposite: focusing on customer acquisition without paying attention to customer experience factors. This leads to poor customer retention and loyalty and, ultimately impacts on the bottom line, leaving the company vulnerable to its competitors.

The structure, process and use of technology in marketing are all aimed at moving customers from one phase of the marketing process to the next one, with the ultimate aim of making the customers stay with the brand over the long term. Owing to many factors, customers' behaviour is always changing, which is why marketing agility is essential to keep pace with this constant change.

Before we firmly define the term 'agile marketing', let's take a look at how marketing works. The way that marketing planning and execution are currently structured broadly follows the Project Management Institute's concept of triple constraints: time, scope and cost of campaigns are rigidly fixed at the start of the year. Each line of business, channel, and strategy is allocated budget for 12 months, which is reviewed only at the end of that period, thus creating a mindset where people try to spend all their budget before the end of the fiscal year – to allow them to ask for a bigger budget the following year. This is the norm; having funds left over at the end of the year is not regarded as being lean, rather is it interpreted as bad planning. The scope of the campaign is also agreed at the start of the year. For example, 'we spend XXX on digital marketing and YYY on offline marketing, while for B2B teams, ZZZ will be allocated to events and webinars'. The scope of the campaign will not change even if subsequent insights reveal deficiencies in some (or event all) of the channels used. The time frame for marketing campaigns in some instances is rigidly set at 12 months. Sure, there are review meetings at the end of each quarter, but these do not necessarily lead to budgets being reallocated from less impactful campaigns to better performing ones. In Chapters 2 and 4, we will go on to discuss ways to improve all aspects of the marketing team to create overall business agility that radiates from within the marketing team.

What is agile marketing? According to Simon Wood, Marketing Director at Clearvision, agile marketing is a collaborative and structured approach to managing marketing campaigns and teams. The approach focuses on adaptive, responsive and iterative strategies as opposed to over-planned, rigid programmes with little to no wiggle room. In its purest form, agile marketing is about using data over opinions and building flexible campaigns on the foundations of cooperation and continuous improvement. Agile is a concept borrowed from software-development teams. The iterative approach of agile in software guarantees a higher product success rate precisely because it is based on tailoring team activities to customers' feedback in order to cater to customers' needs. This is why companies such as Spotify, Google and Netflix have all adopted some form of an agile way of working. Most of the agile marketing practices have been borrowed and adapted from the Agile Manifesto and from frameworks like Scrum, Kanban and, most famously, the Spotify model. Much of the content of this book is based on my conversations with agile marketing executives who are currently using agile methodologies in their marketing-campaign planning and execution and from our discussions so far one common observation emerges: marketing teams that do not adopt agile will not be able to meet customers' changing expectations.

Agile marketing is an optimized approach to people, processes and tools in marketing planning and execution, in response to changing customer behaviour and market trends. It provides a way to respond to these changes by adding, removing and/or modifying marketing targets and strategies on an ongoing basis. Agile marketing focuses on a change in business mindset away from the traditional marketing structure to a more flexible (agile) structure that has been so successful in the IT software industry. It champions data-driven marketing decision making, with an emphasis on value creation from a customer's perspective. In Chapter 2, we will discuss in greater depth how to change the mindset of marketing teams in order to embrace the core values of agile.

Marketing planning and execution are often chaotic activities, characterized by assumptions about the customers, where HIPPO opinions form the bulk of planning decisions. Plans are created without the qualitative insight of customers and without the flexibility of adapting these plans to ever-changing customer perceptions and expectations. This approach worked well before technology influenced marketing reach and empowered customers in their decision-making process. Although marketing planning frameworks have been around for a long time, it is obvious that most of the planning frameworks were developed for bureaucratic, top-down command-and-control environments. While companies such as Google and other social-media platforms have revolutionized marketing reach and campaign reporting, the overall planning model for marketing has largely remained unchanged. Agile marketing was developed as a reaction to changing customer expectations and the need for an adaptive process for campaign planning and execution. The agile marketing mindset welcomes iterative changes to the agreed marketing plan every quarter, or even monthly, depending on the insights obtained from qualitative and quantitative analytics. The goal is to create a customer-oriented mindset by listening to customers and identifying what could be done better to improve the overall customer experience. The marketing budget should be adjusted as necessary to ensure that its emphasis is on providing high value to each customer segment in each channel. In other words, marketing plans should be driven by customer insights, not by available budgets alone.

It is normal for C-level marketing executives to prioritize up-front planning of marketing campaigns before approving budgets for each fiscal year. This approach will work only if it is possible to know with 100% certainty that customer and competitor behaviour will not change during this 12-month period and that there will be no innovations in marketing technology in the meantime. Of course, we all know that there is no 100% certainty in today's business environment. An agile marketing team that embraces adaptive planning continues to learn more about customers and make the necessary adjustments throughout the year. Such a marketing team will not have exactly the same mindset at the end of the year because they will always learn something new about how to improve customer experience. Over time, the team will discover what works and how to alter their strategies to give customers what they want. We will discuss adaptive planning in greater detail in Chapter 4.

Agile marketing emphasizes evolutionary planning and also provides a new challenge to marketing teams to learn how to adjust and align their marketing plans to cater for changing customer behaviour and expectations. In my experience, and from my conversations with agile marketing teams around the world, it is important to move away from the rigid marketing planning approach and to adopt a mindset that encourages listening to customers to inform planning decisions. It essentially means that marketing strategy and planning become more effective as teams learn more about how to improve customer experience through the insights gained from the customer journey map, which is discussed in Chapter 3.

In its common usage, up-front planning of marketing campaigns without the flexibility of adjusting budgets is always likely to be a disaster. A good example is a software company that spent over $400,000 on paid advertising without any tangible results to show from the first quarter, yet their budget for the year was allowed to run until the end of the fiscal year despite evidence showing that the money was being completely wasted. In short, there had been no input from the people who actually executed the campaign into resource allocation decisions. A different kind of problem arises where there are political reasons behind the existence of rigid marketing plans, which can be due to the tension and competition between marketing teams and other lines of the business to get their share of marketing dollars. The agile marketing way to deal with change is to build flexibility into the marketing planning and execution. However, this requires customer insights to inform what kind of marketing strategy would actually increase business revenue and these insights are garnered through customer journey maps. This is not to say that you cannot fix the scope and budget up-front in agile marketing plans. What it does mean, is that the scope and budget should both be updated on a regular basis as a result of customer insights gained. Agility through adaptive planning means that marketing teams continually check the performance of every campaign – and alter the campaign budget and scope accordingly. Doing this will yield better campaign results and a more positive customer experience, because the feedback loop for the marketing-planning strategy is linked to the customer journey map.

Customers' requirements are always changing, which makes monitoring the performance of traditional marketing campaigns extremely difficult, not least because attribution models are technically a waste of time. C-level executives and leadership teams are often too far removed from real-life customers and sometimes rely on external agencies for information. They are more likely to accept the recommendations of consultants over the insights offered by their own internal teams. Customer-facing employees expect marketing plans and strategies to be flexible but are often reluctant to voice their opinion for fear of being perceived to be questioning the vision or marketing strategy of the CMO. Furthermore, what seems like a good marketing plan today, might likely look like a not-so-smart strategy in six months' time due to the ever-changing marketing landscape. A good example of one company being overtaken by another due to not paying attention to their customers and the wider environment is that of Myspace, which was all but obliterated by Facebook in its early days. Your customers will remain loyal only insofar as no competitor can offer a better customer experience at the same price.

Having laid the rationale for the importance of embedding agile within marketing, we move on to explore how agile marketing professionals around the world define the term 'agile marketing'. Michael McKinnon, Global Marketing Operations at Avaya.com, defines agile marketing as a methodology that emphasizes getting tasks and projects completed over adherence to a process. For him, it is a way to rapidly respond to change through quick iterations, rather than being held to one 'grand design'. It is a philosophy that breaks down silos and stresses individual interactions, while considering that many small bets will be more likely to succeed in the long run than will one large bet. In short, it pays homage to the altar of 'done'!

My conversation with Jim Sterne, Founder of eMetrics Summit & Digital Analytics Association, revealed a similar view: he believes flexibility to be the main essence of business agility: keeping track of the numbers, being able to keep track of the marketplace, and reacting to the information gathered in an iterative way. Jim also suggests dividing up a marketing budget by marketplace and not necessarily by channel and passionately advocates the devolution of budgetary responsibility from senior management level down to relevant individuals responsible for executing marketing campaigns. Giving the authority to manage budgets by moving money around based on the performance of each customer segment in each channel puts the control of the money closer to the actual people who execute campaigns – and away from senior management, who are always far removed from the actual execution of marketing campaigns.

Sean Sheppard, of GrowthX Academy, says agile marketing is about designing campaigns that are small, iterative and which focus on testing the performance of each channel, rather than investing in campaigns for specific channels just because everyone else is doing so. For him, successful agile marketing comes from a team focus on agile thinking, which a lot of the traditional campaigns do not have. Most C-level executives believe that their current planning and execution process of marketing is working and they don't see a reason to make any changes. In a similar vein Dave Dame, Agile Leader at Scotiabank, defines agile marketing as: 'Listening to the changing demands of customers and pivoting campaign strategy and execution to maintain alignment with customer expectations'. We live in an age where we can quickly gather customer feedback about the effectiveness of marketing campaigns. Dave believes that this provides marketing teams with the ability 'to pivot like never before', resulting from insights available through qualitative and quantitative analytics. He also believes that agile marketing is about getting marketing teams out of their silos and working closely with product teams and with the people creating solutions that marketing teams are tasked to market. No longer is it a hand-off between product and marketing, but rather it involves continuous collaboration between these teams. In addition to this collaboration, the use of analytics for ongoing alignment of strategy is another factor that makes agile marketing a critical element of business survival. The collective agility of people, processes and technology to improve marketing performance is how I define agile marketing. This means making the planning and execution of the marketing campaign visible to everyone within the organization with the aim of exposing process delays and obstacles that are hindering the effective execution of campaigns. Ultimately, agile marketing is as much about the mindset, as it is about the methodology. Its goal is to improve our learning capability, efficiency, integration, and adaptability to change in order to create and deliver value to customers above all else. Teams that adopt an agile mindset have a collaborative culture that boosts team morale by creating a positive working environment. This makes for an exciting company culture, already adopted by the likes of Google, establishing an environment that people enjoy being a part of. This is what I admire the most about agile.

Important agile marketing concepts

The urge to become agile in marketing depends on our interpretation of the word 'agile'. Although this word was borrowed from IT software development, its application in the context of marketing is slightly different from its use in IT. Agile marketing is the continuous improvement of marketing teams' processes, their team members and technology as a means to increase their customers' overall experience, which directly impacts on business revenue. Although the introduction of technology into marketing has increased the pace of the customer purchase path, decision making and touch points at which customers interact with brands, marketing planning and execution need to be flexible (i.e. agile) enough to adapt to these fast-changing market trends and thus take advantage of emerging market opportunities before their competitors beat them to it. This need for flexibility is, again, similar to the way in which you might plan your relationship when you meet someone new: you are not immediately going to create an entire plan of how you want to live your life and how many kids you want to have. Instead, you start with a short-term plan and then readjust your plan based on your interaction with the other person. Agile marketing attempts the same approach by starting with short-term plans, learning, and then readjusting the plans to eliminate mistakes. Insights and feedback gathered at the end of each sprint are used to readjust the plan for the next sprint to keep the marketing plan flexible and responsive. This iterative planning promotes early identification of any risks involved with the implementation of marketing campaigns by delivering early feedback from the team at the end of each sprint. We will present the agile marketing planning and implementation process in more detail in Chapter 4.

Transparency

Everyone in the team must be able to understand how their work aligns with the team's objectives as well as with the overall company mission. This will not be possible if the culture of the team does not encourage open transparency. Information about the what, why and when of every individual's task must be visible to everyone in the team, in order to understand dependencies between different teams and departments. This helps to reveal frictions and obstacles to task completion and allows for open discussions about how teams and individuals can work together to reduce any delays that they encounter with task completion.

Transparency allows all facets of the marketing plan or activity to be observed by everyone in the team. It also promotes an easy flow of information to all internal and external stakeholders, and an environment that creates an open culture of collaboration. It is important that such information is accessible to everyone in the team. Transparency of all customer feedback, across all customer touch points, and across all departments must be encouraged. Collaboration tools such as JIRA Software and Rally Software can be used as a central repository for all the campaign information and the team's task information. Everyone within the team is granted unrestricted access to all the information in the repository. Agile marketing teams create visual boards that show the list of tasks everyone is currently working on, as well as completed tasks that have been passed on to the next person. All team members must share information about the marketing channels they are responsible for, in order to maintain a uniform understanding of how each channel can combine towards achieving the overall marketing objectives.

Inspection

Agile marketing provides senior members of the marketing team with the opportunity to inspect the quality of tasks being completed as they relate to the agreed KPIs stated in the marketing plan. Inspection is a critical activity that helps the team to identify hindrances and problems that could be hampering the team's efforts towards completing their marketing tasks. In Chapter 4, we will discuss daily meetings and an adaptive planning approach that encourages continuous updating of the marketing plan.

Adaptation

Agile marketing teams participate in four events to inspect and adapt team tasks and activities, to ensure that team members do not deviate from the goal of each sprint. These four events are: daily meetings, sprint planning, sprint reviews, and retrospectives. In Chapter 4 we will discuss the importance of agile rituals and how they allow teams to examine the status and quality of their marketing campaigns. The customer insights available from analytics inform team members about campaign performance, which enables all team members to make the necessary adjustments to their work.

The Agile Manifesto

In this section we will discuss the 2001 *Agile Manifesto* in the context of marketing teams. The objectives of the *Agile Manifesto* are: to create a positive culture by empowering team members; to promote a people-centric approach to marketing to improve collaboration between individuals and other departments; to reduce any waste of time during campaign execution by identifying and removing internal and external bureaucratic impediments to task completion; to increase the value generated from marketing campaigns by ensuring that an insightful customer-feedback loop is established; to create trust and respect between senior management and the marketing team. The *Agile Manifesto* in the context of marketing contains four simple principles:

>> Individuals and interactions over process and tools;

>> Customer collaboration over HIPPO method;

>> Adaptive marketing plan over rigid marketing plan;

>> Autonomy over command-and-control leadership style.

Based on my experience of working in agile marketing teams and through insights gained by speaking to other agile marketing practitioners, I can confidently say that agile in the marketing context is totally different from how it is applied to IT software development teams. As a result, the focus of this book will be the agile values, principles and mindset that are relevant in the context of marketing and other non-IT teams.

Individuals and interactions over processes and tools

The importance of collaboration between team members can never be overemphasized. In my research about how special forces teams in the military operate, I realized that every team member's training is geared towards their career path; that is, team members are trained in preparation for the next promotion level. I noticed the striking similarity with the team structure for agile during my conversation with Richard Sheridan of Menlo Innovations: his teams are structured in pairs with the main aim of cutting out errors. The point I am trying to make is that you should employ whatever works for your team in terms of improving collaboration between team members and creating an environment built on trust and respect. At Google this is called psychological safety. It is not enough to have the best marketing tools available if the office politics within your team are preventing people from collaborating. If the people within your marketing team don't buy into the overall marketing plan and strategy from senior management, how effectively would they be able to use the marketing tools at their disposal?

Agile practices understand that a team is made up of different individuals with different ways of thinking – and often with different aspirations for their careers. This is why the agile marketing framework includes such activities as daily meetings, sprint planning and sprint-review meetings to encourage collaboration and interaction between team members.

Marketing people can go wrong when they rely solely on the marketing technology tools available, without acknowledging that the customer purchase-decision process is not always rational. The methodology for analysing the customer experience is described in Chapter 3, and it includes the ways in which agile marketing teams can leverage qualitative insight towards achieving total marketing agility. The stack of re-targeting, personalization, SEO, CRO and marketing automation tools can sometimes cause you to destroy your relationship with customers if you keep targeting the same set of customers with different tools. How the team works together to achieve a shared vision – without any duplication of efforts – is more important than focusing on tools alone.

Customer collaboration over the highest-paid person's opinion (HIPPO)

Agile marketing is based on creating a customer feedback loop by focusing on the customers rather than relying on the opinions and assumptions of senior management. A customer-first approach is required; don't let your team get drawn into internal squabbles to prove who is the smartest person in the room. This is how it works under the HIPPO approach: decisions about marketing strategy and budget allocation to different channels are influenced by the highest-paid person's opinion (HIPPO) without consultation with the marketing team members who are responsible for executing these campaigns. Everyone is invited into a meeting and told how much budget they get for the year. Leadership teams do not ask for anyone's input or opinion in any shape, way or form, and team members are often too scared to offer their opinions for fear of being sidelined. No team member is therefore involved in the key decision making about the marketing plan and overall strategy. This approach to decision making is extremely counter-productive, as illustrated by the highly publicized demise of Enron in recent times.

One way in which agile marketing teams can put customer collaboration first is by relying on qualitative and quantitative insights generated from web analytics and by customer-service teams that are external to the marketing function. Customers are the lifeblood of any business – ignoring their input when making marketing decisions will result in an increased cost of both customer acquisition and retention. How do we market products to customers if we fail to listen to them and take their opinions on board when creating and implementing marketing campaigns? While web analytics provide some answers, they do not measure customer experience. Later on, in Chapters 3 and 4, we will discuss how agile marketing teams can integrate customer insights and feedback into campaign planning and execution.

Adaptive marketing plan over rigid marketing plan

Less than 20 years ago, marketing communication to the customer went primarily in one direction. Companies advertised on billboards, newspapers, radio and television. The customer was able to access information only through a static medium. This allowed marketing teams to create 12-month marketing plans without the need for any interim updating on account of customers' lack of choice and ability to do any meaningful research. This rigid planning method worked perfectly well for that era because customers had such limited access to product information – there were no social-media platforms and no smartphone apps through which to share purchase experiences. Unfortunately for marketing teams, customers now have virtually unlimited access to information; not only can they compare product information online, they can also share their experiences online. The recent scandal involving a major manufacturer of smartphones is a good example – it resulted in billion dollars losses in revenue. It should therefore be emphasized that flexibility in planning is essential; it is a recipe for disaster to stick rigidly to a 12-month marketing plan and budget allocation that precludes any flexibility.

It is not uncommon for the senior leadership in marketing teams to resist making changes to a marketing plan because it comes across as questioning their competence to create effective and efficient marketing plans. For example, there has recently been a lot of emphasis on allocating substantial marketing budget to paid search and online advertising campaigns by default, which makes it mandatory to include such channels in marketing plans. What happens if your customers are not expecting you to engage with them online? What if your most-valuable customers expect you to interact with them at conferences or face-to-face industry events? What if your team gets relevant insights from web analytics and customer feedback only after the marketing plan has being signed off and approved by senior management? Surely in all these instances a change would be required for the marketing plan to adapt to the customer insights. Would senior management respond to this development and approve an updated marketing plan, or would they simply dig their heels in to save their professional reputation at the expense of the company? If there is no prior agreement that the marketing plan will be subject to change on an ongoing basis, it becomes difficult, if not impossible, for such a marketing team to be truly agile.

Autonomy over command-and-control leadership style

Companies such as Airbnb, Google and WhatsApp all started with a positive culture that encouraged respect towards employees by granting them autonomy and empowered them to provide input into key decision-making processes. This is one of the main reasons why agile teams have been so successful; team members contribute their insights and experience as part of the decision-making process that impacts the team's objectives. The command-and-control approach to leadership creates a negative culture, which fosters the toxic culture of office politics. The whole aim of agile is to encourage inclusive decisions across the entire team without excluding any contributions from junior-level members of the marketing team. Agile marketing teams are T-shaped, being made up of individuals who are continuously developing by acquiring new skills to expand their expertise. Being T-shaped reduces the need to rely on the input of senior management. Having people with multiple skill sets in different marketing channels and strategies will in itself bring about a collaborative and creative atmosphere, while also avoiding the situation where there is just a single person with a particular skill in the team.

The agile marketing principles

Marketing aims to communicate the value proposition of products and services to customers with an emphasis on how their problems (pain points) will be resolved in both the purchase process and subsequent use of those products and services. Continuous customer satisfaction is the main objective of agile marketing teams. As obvious as this may seem, marketing teams have often forfeited customer trust due to a lack of acknowledging customers' emotions. Making assumptions about what customers want without listening to or observing them remains a problem. What is needed is regular communication with customers to understand their requirements and how these requirements are constantly changing. As a marketing professional, when was the last time you had a detailed face-to-face conversation with your company's existing customers? Customer research is discussed in Chapter 3, but it is important to highlight here that web analytics data do not provide qualitative information because metrics can never explain people's emotions.

Agile marketing welcomes a mindset that embraces continuous change in terms of planning and team objectives, and in response to the changes in customer perceptions. Technological innovation has increased the speed at which customers share their brand experiences with each other, leaving companies with the difficulty of maintaining communication with their customers across multiple touch points. Although marketing is responsible for creating product awareness and generating customer traffic to both online and offline stores, it has little or no control over aftersales service and customer service departments that handle customer complaints. Based on insights from a customer journey map (which is discussed in Chapter 3), agile marketing teams can align their planning and execution of marketing campaigns with other customer-facing departments within the organization. In most cases, it would be impractical for marketing teams to become involved in aftersales, but working together with customer service teams they can provide valuable customer insights that would not be available by any other means.

Similar to the structure of the special forces teams we mentioned at the beginning of this chapter, agile marketing teams are built around T-shaped marketers who are motivated to learn new skills. These individuals teach and mentor each other as a team to learn from each other's skills in a collaborative manner that also fosters a positive learning culture. Companies such as Google and Apple provide employees with the environment and trust they need to get the job done, which gives them the competitive advantage that their competitors might never attain. Marketing leaders looking to introduce the agile way of working into their organizations need to adopt a culture that creates a positive working environment, while also providing training and development platforms for individuals to improve both their soft and hard skills.

As marketing professionals, we have an ever growing number of virtual and text-based communication tools available to us, from email platforms, to chat and mobile-messaging platforms. Agile marketing prioritizes face-to-face communication over virtual and text-based communication tools to convey information between team members. Research done by Professor Mehrabian, a renowned expert in psychology, showed that 89% of communication is nonverbal, of which 55% is made up of body language and 38% is based on our tone of voice, whereas only 7% of every communication is verbal. To reduce the amount of context lost in communication, agile marketing recommends increased face-to-face communication through a daily meeting, as well as planning and review meetings. This, in turn, reduces the amount of email communication between teams, which also reduces the potential for any misunderstandings arising from misinterpreted email content.

Conclusion

Having spent the past five months sharing experiences with leading agile marketing professionals, one key theme that came out in each and every conversations was the consensus that agile marketing is not restricted to agile methodologies alone. Many organizations focus on creating new job descriptions for Marketing Technologists, thinking that bringing in fresh blood and skill set will be enough to go agile. However, the core of the agile marketing transformation lies in adopting a growth mindset which will support continuous learning and acquisition of new skills within the marketing team (e.g. coding skills, UX, business analysis, design thinking, Lean, Scrum and any others) and improve the team's ability to deliver value and increase business revenue. However, in order to really benefit from agile, organizations must recognize that marketing is the responsibility of the entire organisation, because every department within it (and not just marketing) has a direct impact on customer experience. We will discuss more about alignment in Chapter 3 and how the organisation should create a holistic view of customer journey from the very first time they engage with a organisation and all through the entire customer lifecycle. But before we move on to alignment, in the next chapter we explore the journey of becoming agile, with an emphasis on emotional intelligence and soft skills of individuals within the marketing team as vital ingredients of marketing agility.

Chapter 2: Agile Marketing Mindset

What skills are necessary for Agile marketing?

Peter Drucker's famous words 'Culture eats strategy for breakfast' highlight the critical role of organizational culture as a prerequisite to the successful implementation of any organizational strategy or process. Google, as one of the most coveted places to work, has taken these words seriously and created the 'Search Inside Yourself' course with the primary aim of developing employees' soft skills (emotional intelligence). This course is taken by Google employees as part of their induction and continuous development within the company. However, in order to develop an appropriate organizational culture and really become agile, an organization needs to be aware of the skill sets its employees possess, which form the cornerstone of developing that culture. There are two types of skills every marketing team must have as a prerequisite to becoming agile: hard skills and soft skills.

Before the discussion turns to soft skills, which form the focus of this chapter because of their importance in supporting the adoption of agile, I briefly present the hard skills and their role in marketing.

Hard skills

It is very important for marketing people to develop the 'technical' marketing skills and competences required to be able to improve the customer experience. The core competences required to complete professional marketing tasks can be learned through formal qualifications and training in marketing and all such skills are often encompassed under the term 'hard skills'. Hard skills that are crucial to marketing are teachable through established educational and professional institutions like the Chartered Institute of Marketing, as well as online training platforms such as LinkedIn and Udemy.com.

Agile marketing teams encourage individuals to be generalizing specialists. A generalizing specialist is someone who has hard skills in more than one marketing channel, such as a combination of (for example) SEO, user experience, web design, social media marketing, PPC, content marketing and web analytics skills. These types of individuals have to continuously develop their skill set in order to become full-stack digital marketing professionals. Similarly, there are professionals in offline marketing who, you will find, have skills in a range of offline marketing tactics from broadcast, print and outdoor advertising to traditional direct marketing. Whatever the marketing context, whether it's offline marketing or digital marketing, these 'well-rounded' professionals are also known as T-shaped marketing people.

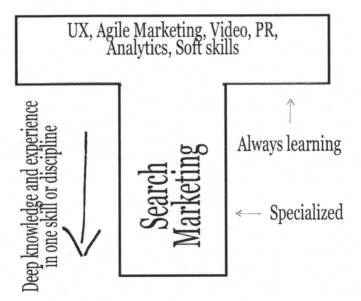

Wide range of basic knowledge

UX, Agile Marketing, Video, PR, Analytics, Soft skills

Deep knowledge and experience in one skill or discipline

Search Marketing

Always learning

←— Specialized

T-shaped marketing professional

Soft skills

Soft skills are the other side of the skills coin. In order to understand the range of soft skills required in the workplace, we need to go all the way back to understanding the development of the human brain. The human brain starts growing from birth with different development stages that continue well into adulthood. We learn to crawl, walk and develop emotional perceptions and attachments to people around us. Parents and caregivers shape our early identity and perceptions about the world in general. However, as we grow and develop, peer pressure and relationships with other people during our formative years shape a significant part of our interpersonal behaviour with others. Some people develop into extroverts and others into introverts. These personality types ultimately impact on the mindset we are likely to adopt both within and outside our workplace.

Research shows that the brain reaches its absolute peak at the age of 22 and then our memory retention starts to decline slowly with less capacity to store and retain information. This is rather scary, considering that most of us only embark on our professional careers at around this age. Alongside this natural biological decline in our brain agility, the stress we experience in our daily lives also impacts on our intellectual performance. Much has been written about endorphins and their role in reducing the stress and pain that builds up in our daily lives, how they can improve our mood and quality of sleep. Because endorphins are released through regular exercise, activities like yoga, meditation and many other types of exercise can have a positive impact on our brain's ability to function, thus improving our mood and reducing the possibility of negative reactions and confrontation in the workplace. Consequently, more and more companies encourage their employees to increase their physical activity through regular exercise by offering gym memberships or other health-related and well-being oriented initiatives as a part of employment incentives.

Have you ever worked with someone who always seems tense and rigid and who always seems to dampen the mood of the people around them in meetings and in other work-related activities? It's not fun and the impact of such behaviour can really affect the rest of the team and spill over into their private lives. Although regular exercise and healthy eating habits can help improve our mood in a positive way, this does not guarantee that our interpersonal skills will be impacted in a positive way as well. Much of that is down to a person's mindset. The implementation of agile marketing starts with developing the appropriate mindset and the only person responsible for this is - you.

Mindset

Mindset is the belief that defines who you are and how you view yourself in the context of work, personal relationships and the wider society. Much of the past research on mindset has claimed that this belief cannot change because our personality is set in stone, it is either positive or negative: there is nothing in between. New research, however, indicates that many aspects of the brain that impact our mindset can be altered well into adulthood. This notion contrasts with the previous scientific consensus that the brain develops during a critical period in early childhood and then remains relatively unchanged or static. It is now known that our brain has an outstanding ability to change and organize its neural pathways based on our ongoing life experiences. The first step to understanding and changing your mindset is to identify which type of mindset you have: is it a *fixed mindset* or a *growth mindset*? The second question to ask is: how do I change my mindset to become agile? To answer these questions we need to delve a little deeper into the research about mindset.

New York Times best-selling author, Dr Carol Dweck, in her recent book *Mindset*, highlighted two possible mindsets a person can have as:

» Growth Mindset (Positive)

» Fixed Mindset (Negative)

The key difference between the two mindsets lies in how a person organizes their work and how they deal with errors and setbacks. People with a fixed mindset believe they are superior and possess attributes that make them better than the people around them. They also believe they don't need to work hard to complete any task. On the other end of the spectrum are people with a growth mindset who believe that their skills and ability can and will be improved with hard work and who never allow stereotypes to prevent them from achieving their personal or career aspirations.

According to Dweck, the positive praise and affirmation of our intelligence that we receive during our early childhood shape the type of mindset we eventually adopt in adulthood. Her research uncovers insights about how parents' remarks on their children's successes can impact the way that the children view themselves. Reportedly, children who were being told they were smart, bright and naturally special ended up having a fixed mindset because they come to believe they *are* superior to other children around them. Children like this were more likely to grow up to become bullies in a bid to feed the assertion of themselves as being special; they naturally feel the urge to undermine other people in order to feel superior. Furthermore, they start deriving pleasure from asserting their superiority by making other people feel bad about themselves which turns into a vicious cycle.

This is not to say that there is anything wrong with parents praising certain characteristics of their children in response to their academic or sporting achievements. It is a well-established fact that children love and respond well to being praised for their efforts when they get good grades at school or finish at the top of their class or excel during sporting activities. Whilst this is a perfectly acceptable way of nurturing a child's self-esteem, we need to be mindful of what it is we praise children for. Dweck's research revealed the potential consequence that labelling a child smart and superior creates in their mindset: despite helping to build up their self-esteem, it can often prove detrimental as children learn to think of themselves as special and the moment they are faced with circumstances that challenge the 'I am special' self-image they lose confidence and motivation to continue with the task at hand. Therefore, praise should be offered for effort, persistence and hard work, i.e. qualities a child can adopt and develop, rather than on the innate biological characteristics a child has little to no control over.

We can all agree that a lot of the issues caused by racism, homophobia and sexism stem from the perception of groups of people that they are somehow special and naturally better than other people. Such societal issues more than likely originate from children's perception of themselves and others, as well as behaviour learnt from their parents and people around them while growing up, which translates into how they approach with these types of situations when they come up. There is one key issue with focusing on praising children for their innate characteristics, according to Dweck: not only does it not improve their confidence, but rather it creates a negative mindset by making these children feel less adequate and act less efficiently when faced with situations that severely test their innate abilities.

> *'If parents want to give their children gifts, the best thing they can do is teach their children to love challenges, be intrigued by mistakes, enjoy effort and keep learning. That way children don't have to be slaves to praise. They will have a lifelong way to build and repair their confidence'*

> *Carol Dweck*

Dweck's research revealed that people who get praised for their intelligence – rather than for their efforts and the hard work they put into getting results – are the ones most likely to develop a fixed mindset and a feeling of general superiority. Such a mindset in the workplace is toxic and can have a detrimental impact on that person's immediate team, as well as on the wider culture of the organization.

Growth mindset

In her book, *Mindset*, Dweck argues that the core of the growth mindset lies in the belief that every person can cultivate their basic qualities through focused effort. People with a growth mindset zero-in on identifying the key qualities they have (or ones that they would like to possess) and have a willingness to exert a concerted effort to develop the required skill to the maximum. As a result, they become more skilled, more effective and more efficient in completing their tasks; they produce results faster and these are often of better quality. Rather than feeling intimidated, growth-oriented individuals usually thrive during the most challenging times at work and do not get involved in the 'blame game' but focus on coming up with solutions to pressing problems. People with a growth mindset are intellectually curious, possess high emotional intelligence and will generally identify with the following statements:

» Failure is an opportunity to grow.

» I can learn to do anything I want.

» Challenges help me to grow.

» My effort and attitude determine my abilities.

» Feedback is constructive.

» I am inspired by the success of others.

» I like to try new things.

People with a growth mindset embrace their mistakes and failures as learning opportunities that will help them avoid making the same mistakes again. They do not pass judgement on themselves or others in relation to the way they deal with problems and issues they encounter in their work and personal life. Growth mindset enables individuals to welcome challenges at work because they understand that challenges will improve their skills and help them develop to become better at their job. This mindset also enables them to understand and accept their strengths and weaknesses in their professional lives and to identify appropriate ways not only to strengthen their skills in areas they are most knowledgeable about, but also to develop the skills they need to eliminate their areas of weakness. Individuals with a growth mindset continuously and actively seek out constructive criticism from their colleagues and do not allow criticism to affect the confidence they have in their own ability to improve with hard work. They don't take offence and don't tend to hold a grudge against people who offer negative feedback to them about their performance.

Growth mindset is about simply not accepting that you have any limitations as to how much you can develop your hard and soft skills as a marketing professional. It is, ultimately, the belief that your current intelligence, skills, talent are just a starting point on your journey through life, and that all of these can be improved through further training and development – in whichever direction you want to take your life and career. Marketing people who employ a growth mindset are passionate about learning new skills and developing their individual abilities. Hence, they are much more likely to embrace the agile approach because they will not be discouraged by failure while completing marketing tasks, rather are they likely to consider them as an important learning process that leads to ongoing improvements.

The 2016 Scrum guide (Scrum framework) highlights the need for agile teams to possess values such as courage, focus, commitment, respect and openness as part of the mindset required to be agile. From an agile marketing perspective, having a growth-oriented mindset can be compared to creating a learning road map for your career by continually adding new skills as you discover your weaknesses in terms of career-development opportunities. We are all aware of professional athletes like Michael Jordan who were able to shape their life and career by believing that success is not achieved as a birthright, but through learning from their own mistakes and working hard to correct these and improve their skills.

Growth Mindset

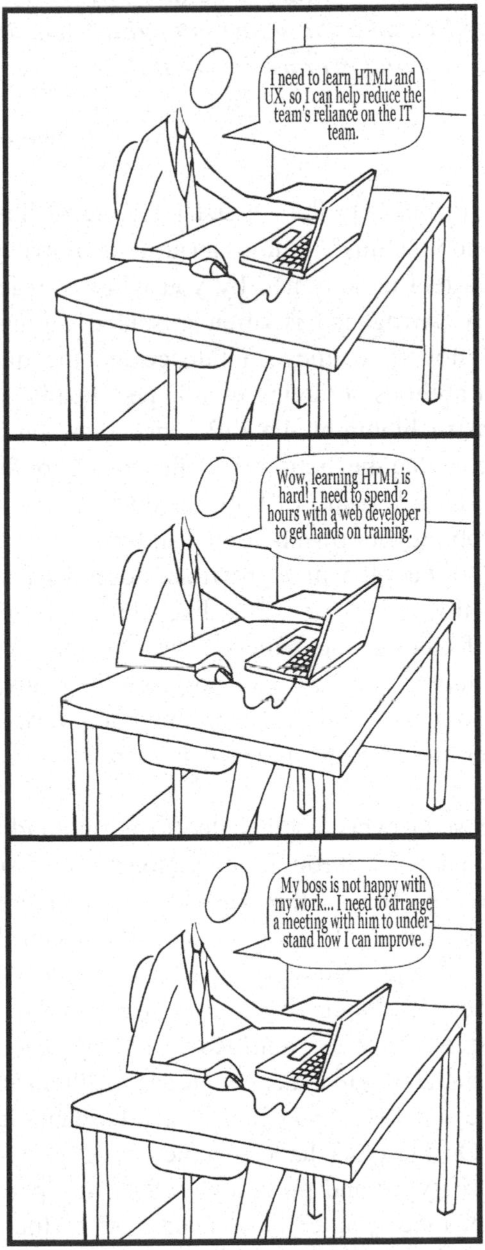

*'I've missed more than nine thousand shots in my career,
I've lost almost three hundred games. Twenty-six times I've
been trusted to take the game-changing shot and missed.
I've failed over and over again in Life'*

Michael Jordan

Arrogance is attributed to the superstar feeling of being superior to everyone around you; this promotes an attitude of irritation both ways because people feel undermined by you while you feel irritated by their inferiority. Arrogance is often mistaken for confidence. The Cambridge dictionary defines confidence as 'the quality of being certain of your abilities or having trust in people, plans or the future'. It is important to highlight the difference between arrogance and confidence – note that the dictionary definition of confidence contains the words 'trust' and 'respect', both for oneself and for others. The belief in developing your own potential and that of people around you is the hallmark of people with a growth mindset. Real self-confidence is reflected in the actions of CEOs like Steve Jobs, Bill Gates and the founders of Google and Zappos. These people all have one key element in common: they all want to grow their business and they believe they can achieve this only through hard work and respect for their employees and other people around them.

Stereotypes exist in every society due to norms and traditions that have been passed down through generations; issues such as racism, sexism and homophobia in the workplace can severely disrupt the performance of individuals who are subject to such discrimination. We can agree that some people believe they are superior to everyone else at work because of their 'Ivy League mentality' or their top-class university degrees; they feel entitled to having the best ideas and suggestions, which tends to make people around them accept whatever suggestions they make – even if they are fundamentally wrong or ill-conceived. On the other hand, people with a growth mindset are immune to stereotypes and they never allow any perceptions about their education, race, gender or sexuality affect their performance at work. They believe that any skill can be developed through hard work and they are honest with themselves about personal weaknesses that they need to eliminate. Growth-mindset individuals are always the first to accept challenging tasks at work because they cherish the opportunity to learn from difficult tasks.

Fixed mindset

A fixed mindset is the belief that your natural intelligence, skills and talent are all set at birth. People with this mindset believe that nothing can be done to increases or improve their skills because they think they are naturally smart and do not need any improvement, they are confident in their existing skills and feel compelled to prove these over and over again. Marketing people with a fixed mindset are often heavily involved in 'dirty' office politics because they feel comfortable in their role and do not usually perceive a need to improve themselves by acquiring new marketing skills - hard or soft. They will often take on tasks they are comfortable with and can easily complete, just to reinforce their intelligence. To find out if you have a fixed mindset, ask yourself this question: do I always want to show people how smart I am or demonstrate that I am smarter than everyone else in my marketing team?

It is fair to conclude that marketing people who actively resist adopting the agile marketing methodology have a high likelihood of possessing a fixed mindset. Think about it: is there a person within your team who hoards information and keeps it from other members of the team? Is there someone within the team who gossips and spreads rumours or who blocks creative ideas from materializing? These types of individuals hinder agile marketing adoption within teams. Bad bosses and toxic people most of us encounter in the workplace are perfect examples of individuals with a fixed mindset. People with a fixed mindset cannot accept criticism and they feel hurt when they receive corrective or constructive feedback about their performance at work. They are scared to face challenges because these could lead to failure and they have a strong belief that they are too good to fail. After all, in

their opinion a talented person should not be part of a failed project. These individuals will often identify with the following statements:

» Failure is the limit of my abilities.

» I am either good at it or I am not.

» My abilities are unchanging.

» I can either do it or I can't.

» I don't like to be challenged.

» My potential is predetermined.

» When I am frustrated, I give up.

» Feedback and criticism are personal.

» I stick to what I know.

In the twenty-first century, influenced by the shift from interruption to permission marketing, marketing teams must change from traditional demand and control (fixed) mindset towards better customer experience mindset, if they are to survive in today's marketing arena. Embracing a growth mindset will help marketing teams fulfil their potential of achieving increased business revenue whilst supporting the delivery of a healthy customer experience, thus justifying their existence to the rest of the organization and (particularly) the C-suite executives.

Some marketing people by default have a rigid mindset that aligns perfectly with the hierarchical company structure, which favours the waterfall project management framework. This works well in marketing campaigns where we are able to predict outcomes. However, it can be a huge hindrance if the organization wants to be flexible and able to respond to the needs of its consumers quickly and effectively – in other words, if it wants to be agile. Developing a flexible mindset that will support this transition from the waterfall to the agile marketing framework, however, requires a culture of openness that encourages mistakes to be made in order to allow teams to learn from these and improve for the future. Responsibility for developing the culture of an agile organisation ultimately lies with its leadership. However, this culture must permeate the entire organization – and not just its marketing function.

People with a fixed mindset tend to believe in stereotypes and always have a superiority notion about themselves. They believe they are born with special attributes that enable them to exert less effort to complete a task than other 'normal' people would; they don't believe they need to improve anything about themselves because ever since their childhood they have always been told they are smart or have been born with a permanent 'smart gene'. Such individuals are also extremely judgemental about people around them; they don't believe their colleagues are either naturally special or naturally extraordinary. They cannot participate in efforts that lead to the success of other people because they view the success of colleagues as threats to their own superiority and brilliance. Have you ever worked with someone who is always quick to blame someone else or something else when they encounter problems? Do they always have a ready excuse as to why it is not their fault that problems arose with a marketing campaign? People with a fixed mindset have very high ego and would rather blame someone else or come up with excuses even if it means they have to lie or be deceitful in the process. They will throw anyone and everyone 'under the bus' to maintain their self-esteem. These individuals cannot handle criticism or negative feedback – they shut down or take things personally when they hear criticism from their colleagues or their line manager.

A fixed mindset discourages learning. It makes an individual believe that learning is for people with less ability. Fixed-mindset types also have little or no motivation to explore ways to improve their learning potential to acquire new skills. Marketing people with a fixed mindset believe that they don't need to try too hard to get the best result in their work. They don't see any need in registering for industry certification or learning new skills because they always assume they are 'thought leaders' and that they do not need to learn anything new because they feel they already know everything.

Companies will often recruit big talents, mostly people with degrees from prestigious universities, which in and of itself is not a bad thing. However, whilst a prestigious degree can (to an extent) guarantee the level of hard skills a person has, unfortunately, this usually comes in a package with a great, big, fixed mindset. The question that springs to mind is: what type of culture do you create when you hire people with a fixed mindset? Enron is a good example of a company that got into trouble after they focused on hiring top, talented people with huge egos and a fixed mindset. Even when things were going terribly wrong at Enron, their senior management refused to acknowledge their mistakes and work towards fixing the issues, because they were more interested in protecting their own egos and self-esteem. They lied to investors and refused to admit they had a serious problem within Enron at the time. We are all well aware of how that situation ended and the repercussions it had for the organization and a range of their external stakeholders.

How to develop the right mindset

To develop the mindset required for agile marketing, the first step is to improve on your soft skills, also known as 'emotional intelligence'.

It is the ability to understand internal feelings as they happen and be able to interpret and process these feelings in order to control our reactions. The second part is the ability to analyse and assess the emotional states and reactions of the people we are interacting with, both in our personal and professional environments. Becoming an agile marketing professional requires significant improvement in your ability to be self-aware - aware of your emotions, of what triggers specific emotional responses and how you can consciously control these. Additionally, you also need to continuously work on being able to recognize and understand other people's emotional states and how these affect your interpersonal relationships with them.

> *'Emotional Intelligence refers to the capacity for recognizing our own feelings and those of others, for motivating ourselves, and for managing emotions well in ourselves and in our relationships.'*

> *Daniel Goleman*

There are numerous schools of thought on the topic of emotional intelligence in the workplace and how it can increase productivity and output in companies such as Google. This is a direct result of its recognised importance in the workplace. Emotional intelligence is known to impact your ability to succeed in work as well as to promote good relationships in your personal life outside the workplace. It is encouraging to know that everyone can develop their emotional intelligence through appropriate training, the right approach and, most importantly, a strong willingness to improve. Below I present the agile marketing mindset as it relates to soft skills (emotional intelligence) under two categories: intrapersonal emotional intelligence, and interpersonal emotional intelligence.

Improving your intrapersonal emotional intelligence

Have you ever sent an email in the heat of the moment or responded to a colleague in a rude way when they said something you perceived as a direct attack, all the time being painfully aware that you have no ability to control your thoughts or actions? You are not alone – it happens to many people and often. This is a clear example of a harmful lack of self-awareness. Daniel Goleman defines self-awareness as 'knowing one's internal states, preferences, resources and intuitions'. The first stage of developing intrapersonal emotional intelligence is centred around developing your self-awareness capabilities. This is more than just knowing whether you are introvert or an extrovert. Self-awareness is not just about accepting that you 'have a short temper' or it 'takes you a while to explode in anger'. You need to make an active effort to understand how your mind works and what triggers your emotions in a positive or negative way. In order to change the way you deal with your emotions, you first need the ability to be in touch with your emotions and to monitor them so that you can channel them into your thinking in a calm, logical and rational way. You need to be able to identify your emotional state and take control of it, so that you don't say or do anything you will regret. You can start by asking yourself the following questions: Do I have a big ego and how does my ego affect my emotions? How do my emotions affect my self-confidence? What triggers specific negative emotional responses? How do I judge other people's actions around myself at work? Do I feel irritated when someone has competing goals or disagrees with me about marketing strategy? Your emotions are often inextricably tied up with past experiences and the beliefs and values that you have learnt from childhood. Therefore, you first need to first acknowledge your emotional reactions to such incidents at work and then decide how you want to respond and what would be the most intelligent way to react. You might not have control over how people behave in their professional relationships with you but you most definitely can control what you feel and how you react to such unpleasant situations.

Intrapersonal Emotional Intelligence

Self-awareness

The first stage to achieving self-awareness is attention training, which helps you understand your physical reaction when you are angry or upset. How do you recognize it? Do you start sweating when you get angry? Does your breathing get faster or does your voice start to crack? Physical reactions to emotions such as anger are different in everyone: some people go silent when they are angry, whilst others start screaming at the top of their voice. You need to be able to understand reactions that happen in your body before you get angry or upset. Identifying these reactions will help you focus on how to deal with them so that you can remain calm and in control.

Apart from recognising the physical reactions to the emotions you are experiencing, attention training also involves actively listening to your inner thoughts and focusing your attention on your interpretations of events around you and of other people's interaction with you. For example, someone might have different personal values or poor communication with you. In these situations, it's very easy to conclude that such individuals are being rude and disrespectful towards you and you could easily conclude that they are trying to undermine you. Have you ever had a direct report who is always providing solutions to all problems that arise at work? Have you ever felt a sense of envy or resentment towards that person? All these things can go on in your mind without us even noticing or realizing this type of toxic behaviour emanates from us. Some individual self-awareness will often go a long way in repairing negative work environments, even without implementing any official changes within the team. Self-awareness is the process by which you search inside yourself to identify different emotions you feel in different situations. Self-awareness and attention training can help us identify our internal thought processes and how they impact on our mindset. This then gives you the opportunity to be more self-aware and channel your behaviour in a positive and collaborative way that helps the team. It is important to be able to understand when our emotions are triggered by our own judgements about other people's actions towards us. When someone does not say 'good morning' to you in the corridor and then they arrive late to a meeting, do you get angry because they arrived late or because they didn't say 'good morning'? Do you ask a clarifying question to ascertain why they arrived late to the meeting or do you just pass judgement about their tardiness without bothering to find out exactly what the reason for it was?

Your emotions are yours alone and nobody can make you feel angry. Be aware of your range of emotions and what triggers them. Be aware of what type of people, comments, conversations or situations trigger negative emotional reactions within you and try and understand why they always trigger such negative emotions. This is the first step to changing your mindset.

The reason self-awareness is so important in changing your mindset is because being able to acknowledge your inner self also improves your ability to empathize with other people, and this is crucial for improving relationships with others, whether personal or professional. Having empathy means having the ability to understand other people's emotions or situations they find themselves in; it means walking a mile in their shoes and looking at things from their perspective. Honesty and confidence are prerequisites to having empathy: once you improve your self-awareness you are able to replace your inner thought process with the other person's views and analyse how you would feel if you were in their situation.

Google, as the archetypal agile company, familiarizes its employees with the concept of attention training through a three-week course called 'Search Inside Yourself', which is led by Chade-Meng Tan. In his book (also titled Search Inside Yourself) Meng asserts that 'Meta-attention is attention to attention, ability to pay attention to attention itself. Simply put, meta-attention is the ability to know that your attention has wandered away'. Therefore, when you are able to listen and pay attention to your emotions as they occur, you increase your ability to control these emotions with the same skill and ease as those required to drive a car. You can see and sense everything around you whilst still being in perfect control.

So, the next time you notice your mood changing at work or at home, pause for a moment and focus your wandering mind on what is causing your emotions to change or the specific reason why you are becoming angry or sad. Ask yourself: Does my change in mood affect people around me? When I raise my voice to a colleague or subordinate in a meeting, what impact does that have on them individually and on the rest of my team? These self-awareness exercises will help you pay more attention to your emotions and be accountable for how your actions can affect others. The best way to improve the quality of your attention training in a bid to understand your internal emotions is through 'Mindfulness Meditation', which Jon Kabat-Zin defined as 'paying attention in a particular way: on purpose, in the present moment and nonjudgmentally'. I would recommend researching and reading more about mindfulness and meditation to improve your attention training skills. See the Further Reading section for recommended reading about mindfulness and meditation.

Self-awareness plays a big part in developing a growth mindset (as presented earlier in this chapter), but unfortunately it is not always possible to be 100% self-aware of your emotions all of the time. This is why it is important to get constructive feedback from people around you about how you behave and react towards them in specific situations, as well as what they think you could improve on in order to create better relationships with them. Although this might make you uncomfortable or even slightly embarrassed, the benefits of going through this process can be plentiful and positively affect not just your relationships with others within your team, but also the corporate culture of the organization for which you work.

Self-control

Daniel Goleman has described self-control as self-regulation or 'handling our emotions so that they facilitate, rather than interfere, with the task at hand', 'being conscientious and delaying gratification to pursue goals' and 'recovering well from emotional distress'. After listening to your inner self and understanding the emotions you are feeling, it is important to learn how to react in a rational way to avoid rash reactions that can lead to regret and have negative consequences for your career and your relationships with your line manager or colleagues. In the previous section we discussed self-awareness and its role in helping you identify the triggers that cause you to have impulsive, emotional reactions. The key is to notice these triggers before and when they occur so that you can restrain yourself from reacting immediately.

One useful technique of self-control involves pausing when you experience a negative emotion and then counting from 1 to 10 while taking deep breaths to ensure that your brain gets enough oxygen. This is important because studies have shown that deep breathing increases the supply of oxygen to the brain, which helps you to take a step back, evaluate and change your initial emotional response. Breathing helps your body and mind relax so that you are better placed to understand your current emotional state; you can then choose a better response to any given situation. It is important to be able to de-escalate the surge of blood that rushes through your body when you get angry. Take a walk and get some fresh air to help take your mind off the issue that triggered your anger. This will also allow you time to review your choices before deciding on any one specific course of action. When you find yourself getting angry, it's important to understand your reason, thought or judgement of the action that triggered your anger: is the story that is making you angry really true, or are you just reacting to your own perception of the situation? Self-control gives you the ability to calm down and ask clarifying questions which help you better understand your own psychological profile.

Why is understanding our psychological profile important? What happens when we try to suppress or ignore our emotions? They come back to bite us in a really epic way. We all have our judgements about different emotions and whether they are inherently positive or negative. The reality is that we will experience a whole range of emotions at different times and the tools of self-awareness and self-control are crucial in enabling us to understand the connection between the raw emotions and our reactions. Once we've got a good grip on our emotions and why we react a certain way to them, it is important to actively understand how our emotions and the resulting reactions are shaped by our own interpretations of other people's actions. Questions are a really powerful tool that can aid us in developing this understanding. Don't make assumptions about people's intentions. Instead, ask questions to find out the truth before you reach any conclusion about people's intentions, get clarification and avoid emotional explosion. It's really important to know how you think about events, identifying those things that trigger your hot button. Is it the perceived unfair treatment from your boss or lack of equal opportunities within the team? How does that shape your response and reaction to such people and how does it affect your relationship with them moving forward?

Another important factor in developing self-control is the quantity and quality of our sleep. Have you ever felt prone to being irritable because you didn't get enough sleep? Some people attribute lack of sleep to being hard-working, which is not necessarily correct. In the same way that cars and equipment need repair, servicing and maintenance for them to function at optimum capacity, most people need to get at least eight hours' sleep to be able to function effectively. Plan your sleep pattern and make sure it is consistent, with a strong emphasis on at least eight hours' sleep per night if possible. Remember, your health is your wealth, so it's your responsibility to look after yourself.

Improve your interpersonal emotional intelligence

Social awareness skills

> *'Handling emotions in relationships well and accurately reading social situations and networks; interacting smoothly; using these skills to persuade and lead, negotiate and settle disputes, for the cooperation and teamwork'*
>
> *Daniel Goleman*

Have you ever experienced excellent customer service from the help

Interpersonal Emotional Intelligence

desk of a company you were not particularly pleased with when you first called to resolve an issue? Where the person talking to you over the phone does not only resolve the issue that made you call customer service in the first place, but seems to know what to do to make your experience actually enjoyable? So much so that, at the end of the discussion, you actually apologize for your angry reaction at the start of the conversation? These companies know that investing in people with a strong social awareness is the key to keeping their customers happy and – more importantly – loyal.

Social awareness is a skill that helps us recognize and understand the mood of other individuals or even entire groups of people. In his book Emotional Intelligence 2.0, Travis Bradberry states that social awareness is 'looking outward to learn about and appreciate others', it is 'centered on your ability to recognize and understand the emotions of others'. Therefore, social awareness has two complementary and interlinked parts. To be able to improve your skill of reading other people's emotions, you first need to be able to listen to your own emotions and identify how they contribute to the way your colleagues react to your emotional reaction to them. This means being able to pay attention to other people, while learning how to understand their body language, tone of voice and facial expression. We all make either rational or emotional decisions based on whatever state of mind we find ourselves in at any particular moment. To be able to control our emotions, we first need to ask ourselves clarifying questions about whether our emotions are causing us to ignore rational decision making. For example, think about how you feel when someone sends you a condescending email or throws you under the bus at work? It is very easy to take offence when we perceive others to be disrespectful towards us and we feel they are being condescending. The same applies to everyone else, which is why it is important to make a point of always being respectful in our interactions with others. Do you pay attention to your body language when you are angry or in an uncomfortable situation? What hand gestures do you make? Do you fold your arms above your chest in front of you or do you keep them in your pockets? Do you respond by immediately defending yourself or launch a verbal attack on the other person, pointing out their mistakes? It is important to pay attention to what people say, as well as their body language when you are communicating with them. Their choice of words and their body language can provide you with both overt and subtle clues that can help you adjust your communication with them to make the interaction more effective.

Now, listening and observing in a communication interaction is important, but it is only the first step. To be able to successfully regulate our emotions we need to employ an active strategy. For example, you could pause and reduce your emotional reaction by analyzing the context of the situation. This should help you to calm down and regain your composure in the heat of the moment. You obviously don't need to make your calming down process obvious to the person whose words or behaviour triggered these emotions inside you, but it is important that you take ownership of it within yourself. Sometimes just pausing and counting 1 to 10 while taking deep breaths might not be enough to help you regulate your emotions and in such situations you can allow yourself a day or two to think about how to respond to the situation that triggered the emotion within you. Time really does help you calm down. Apart from managing your reactions internally, it is also important to try to smile - and a lot! Recent research shows that smiling boosts positive emotions by stimulating your heart rate, blood pressure and other stress-level indicators and this can have a positive impact on improving your emotions internally.

Relationship management skills

Being part of a team requires continuous relationship development with colleagues, your line manager and other stakeholders within the organization. Office politics exist in every organization because it's an inherent trait of humans to compete and form cohorts with people who share their values. Some companies are more toxic than others and to be able to survive this type or organization you need to pay attention to your relationship with the people around you – this means your peers, your superiors and your subordinates alike. Creating a healthy working relationship with people is an ongoing process that requires constant awareness of your emotions and others' emotions in a bid to avoid conflict or confrontations. Relationship management starts with improving your listening skills: even though most people believe they are good listeners, the truth is we could all do with more effective listening from time to time. If you are interested in improving your listening skills, then I would recommend reading the book 'Just Listen' by Mark Goulston.

Getting to know the people around you by asking questions and really listening to them can reveal things about them that will help you understand how to relate to them. However, in order to create a successful relationship, the listening and sharing needs to go both ways: you also need to be willing and able to reveal things about yourself and your personality which will help the people around you know how to relate to you. Some people are introverts but could be mistaken for snobs if they do not explain to people around them that they are introverts – and aware of it.

Communication style is another thing to consider when trying to develop and maintain a positive working relationship with people at work. Some people think Americans tend to be 'loud' whilst other cultures (for example Chinese or Korean) are perceived as being reserved and conservative. Paying attention to your and your colleagues' oral and written communication style can help you avoid conflict resulting from any difference in the contextual interpretation of your words. Although some people employ the strategy of 'kissing-up' or 'kissing-down' to maintain good working relationships with people around them, it is always better to be genuine and offer comments and feedback when they are appropriate and called for. Endeavour to focus on the simple things, for example, saying thank you when someone helps you out with a task at work, or apologizing when you make a mistake that might have a negative impact on another person's performance rating can provide subtle signs that you appreciate your co-workers and are mindful of their needs, time and commitment.

Some research even suggests that we can predict a person's response based on their personality type and thus facilitate more effective communication. Without delving too deep into a discussion of theories of personality, we will just briefly present some of Carl Jung's research which identifies four personality types and classifies people's temperament in terms of four colours:

> » Cool Blue: These individuals live their lives according to the principles, facts and logic that they consider realistic. They are always careful when making decisions because they want to be sure they have explored all the necessary facts before making an informed decision. They are methodical with a structured approach to planning a work task from start to finish.

> » Earth Green: These types of people have high emotional control and are always calm and composed in high-pressure situations. They are skilful in creating and maintaining relationships with others because they possess a high level of empathy, which allows them to show concern for other people's feelings and well-being.

> » Sunshine Yellow: These individuals are goal-oriented with a clear vision of what they want for their career and how to achieve it. They might sometimes come across as daydreamers with unrealistic targets because of their creative imagination ay hope for the nd their hopes for the future.

> » Fiery Red: These people are direct, full of energy and know exactly what they want. They don't allow events of the past to affect their focus for the future. They sometimes appear to be in a hurry and not willing to allow anything to delay them in their career.

Understanding different personality types

Figure 2.3 depicts the significant personality types. We often attribute an individual's personality type according to two whether they are predominantly an introvert, predominantly an extravert, or possibly a mix of both. However, there is more to personality types than that. We will focus in this section on the work of Isabel Myers and Katherine Myers-Briggs, authors of the personality inventory known as the Myers-Briggs Type Indicator (MBTI). It is important to understand your own personality type and those of the people you interact with, if you wish to improve your social-awareness skills and create and maintain healthy working relationships. According to Isabel Myers and Katherine Myers-Briggs, there are four dimensions of personality:

1.   Extraversion vs Introversion

2.   Sensing vs Intuition

3.   Thinking vs Feeling

4.   Judging vs Perceiving

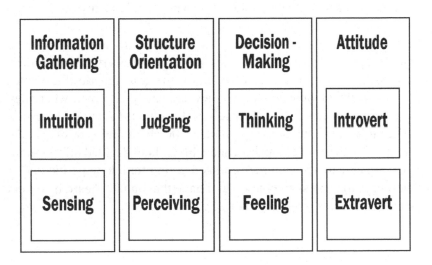

Myers-Briggs Dimensions of Personality

We present each of these in greater detail in the sections below.

Extraversion and introversion

Extraverts explained

Extraverts tend to focus their energies outwards and they enjoy speaking in front of a group. Some people enjoy being around people more than others and extraverts thrive on group activities or anything that allows them to spend time around other people, especially their friends and family. They exhibit a high degree of awareness of the activities going on around them and they naturally blend into new surroundings because they find it very easy to talk to anyone.

Being an extravert does have its negatives in a work context, but increased self-awareness can help an extravert improve their performance. Because extraverts enjoy the camaraderie that comes from spending time with people, they can easily get bored when they have to complete a task by themselves. Extraverts tend to prefer group or team learning and are very enthusiastic about brainstorming; they are quicker than most to make a decision without detailed information; they are able to maintain focus on something for a long period due to their urge to express an opinion and have that opinion heard by others and they process information orally.

Working with extraverts

Creating a good relationship with an extravert requires you to listen to them and talk less because this will give them the impression that you are paying attention and that they are being heard. It's important that you acknowledge and credit their ability to initiate a group conversation or brainstorming session for ideas. Try not to interrupt them when they talk and instead really listen and allow them to explain their opinion in detail. Understand that they like being around people as opposed to being alone, so the next time you notice your extraverted colleague feeling lonely and you are less busy, try giving them some attention by spending time with them – it will have a great impact on their mood and their work performance, whilst at the same time improving the atmosphere within the team.

How extraverts can improve their relationship skills in the workplace

In a business context, it is important to learn how to pause and think before voicing an opinion to avoid saying something you might regret. Phrase the sentence in your mind first and assess the impact it is likely to make, to determine whether there is any possibility your statement could be taken out of context. It is also necessary to recognise when to be silent and when to speak. Extraverts must learn to be silent until they have all the facts before giving their informed opinion. Since extraverts are liable to speak out before they think, how does an extravert (or a naturally talkative person) keep silent in order to listen to what others are trying to communicate? Take heed of the following advice for various situations:

» Be silent when you are provoked to anger.

» Be silent if your words could potentially convey a wrong impression or context and also if you are not sure about what impact your words will have on others.

» The only way for you to listen to and understand others is by actively trying to be silent.

» Be silent if your words will damage or negatively impact the reputation of others.

» Be aware that by dominating a discussion you might be perceived as showing a lack of respect, because you are restricting or preventing others from expressing their opinion.

» Be silent when you or others have work to do because talking takes your concentration away from your work and those you speak to will also then need time to refocus on their work every time you interrupt them.

Introverts explained

Introverts tend to focus their energies inwards and focus their attention on their own inner thought processes. They like being around people they know and have developed a trusting relationship with. They enjoy their privacy and keep their opinions to themselves after thinking things through carefully in their head. They come across as shy when they meet people for the first time and take their time to warm to people. They tend to be silent during team meetings and are less likely to express their opinions during brainstorming sessions. Introverts dislike being asked for an immediate opinion because they need time to process and digest information before making a decision. Unlike extroverts, introverts find it easy to stay focused on their work and can maintain their attention span for longer periods of time.

Working with introverts

Having colleagues who are introverts has tremendous benefits because such people are naturally deep-thinking and less likely to make knee-jerk decisions without first thinking about the pros and cons. This is why it is important to understand that introverts need time to think before committing to something or making a decision; introverts might come across as sluggish but you need to give them time and space to think.

I am introverted and sometimes find it hard to accept invitations to after-work drinks; as a result, I have often been labelled as being cocky and arrogant. As you can imagine, this has impacted on my work relationships and ultimately had an impact on my job satisfaction. Whilst I have, with time, improved on this aspect of my personality, I still find it challenging in new work environments. However, improving my self-awareness and self-management has meant that now people do recognise me as an introvert, rather than someone who is cocky or arrogant. It's important not to pressure introverts to attend absolutely every group social event if their presence is not strictly required. However, in work-related group discussions, when there is a 'loud mouth' who talks more than everyone else in the room, it is important to actively encourage introverts to contribute their opinions. Just be sure to make them aware of the fact that you will be looking for their input during meetings in advance.

How introverts can improve their relationship skills in the workplace

At work we often can't control our immediate environment – it can be loud and noisy when you least expect it to and this is, usually, when you need your concentration the most. Therefore, when feeling stressed from the noise in a crowded office, try finding some 'me time' for yourself to help you relax away from the hustle and bustle. This can be done both during and outside of your working hours. In group meetings and brainstorming sessions, anticipate that you will be called on to offer your input, so do a thorough preparation beforehand and have some notes ready to discuss with the rest of the team. Summon up your courage to speak and volunteer your opinions, rather than wait to be asked to contribute. Do this especially when a 'loud mouth' is becoming the focus and attention of the meeting, but be polite and raise your hand to gesture that you would like to speak rather than interrupting the 'loud mouth'. When invited to after-work events, make the effort to attend once in a while and try to build up a rapport with people from other departments or anyone who is open to a conversation.

Sensing and intuition

Sensors explained

People that fall under this personality category are usually fact-based thinkers with high attention to detail at work. Personal development and learning new skills for these individuals will always be done in a linear and sequential learning pattern because they enjoy a step-by-step approach to learning new things. As practical and realistic people, they base their decision-making processes on current events but they will also rely on their past experience when necessary.

Sensors tend to be direct and blunt when describing things and they sometimes lack diplomacy. They prefer clarity about what is expected of them and dislike vague information that does not give them explicit task requirements. They receive information by using their five natural senses and they assimilate information best through visual and auditory cues, focusing on hard facts and detail to develop their understanding of any given situation.

Working with sensors

Sensors deal in facts when they are trying to communicate information about their decision-making process. In situations when you have an idea and need to get buy-in from a sensor, make sure you communicate your message in a practical way. Present them with facts when trying to communicate a message to them and make sure you back up your statements with evidence or data that can be verified.

How sensors can improve their relationship skills in the workplace

As a sensor, your strength is also your weakness and it is important to learn to sometimes be less practical and more flexible - you do not always have to ask for detailed facts and evidence for every idea presented to you. Understand that not everything can be measured and that it is possible to have working theories without specific data-based evidence to back them up, so keep an open mind about creative ideas that do not have data evidence to validate them. Companies such as Airbnb and Uber started without any data evidence to prove that they would be successful but they developed to become big brands.

Intuitives explained

Intuitives focus on meaning, interpretation and possibilities and they process information using their own intuition. They are keen to try new things and excel at innovative thinking with a focus on the future. The possibility of learning through imaginative and inspirational insights excites them. Prone to multitasking, they are always in a hurry to reach a destination. This can sometimes make them careless with detail, but they will relish any kind of creative and imaginative tasks.

Working with intuitives

Acknowledge their creative thinking and learn to trust their innovative ideas. Try not to burden them with excessive information and data. When involved in a repetitive task, they enjoy adding new tweaks to old ways of working, so you may find that they fuel the innovation within your team – give them the space to do so.

How intuitives can improve their relationship skills in the workplace

The creative and imaginative thinking you possess as an intuitive can sometimes be a problem in the workplace and you need to develop your ability to focus and keep your attention on the task at hand and the reality within which you operate. Find ways to align your creativity and forward thinking with available facts and spend some time turning your creative ideas into real-life working solutions to the problems or issues your team or your organisation is faced with.

Thinking and feeling

Thinkers

Thinkers prefer objective analysis of information and, because they are reasonable and fair, they have a strong sense for justice. Although they might come across as direct and insensitive at times on account of their strong mind, they make up for that by being fair and reasonable. Being calm and composed makes it easy to base decision making around objective data and logical analysis. Furthermore, because they are not interested in 'sucking up' to people or being popular, thinkers focus on the pros and cons of issues and are always keen to understand the logical consequences of any activity or task they are involved in. They lean towards the most reasonable course of action for every task in order to be confident about the results and consequences of their individual, as well as team, actions.

Working with thinkers

Take the time to understand what they are thinking as opposed to how they feel about work-related activities. Team members can tap into their calm personality at times of chaos and this makes them invaluable to every team. Because they focus on issues, rather than people, thinkers are less likely to take things personally, so any disagreements are best brought out into the open to be dealt with immediately.

How thinkers can improve their relationship skills in the workplace

Pay closer attention to your conversations with your colleagues to avoid being branded as unappreciative because of your ability to think deeply. Also, learn to be encouraging towards other people's less thought-out opinions – be constructive in your criticism.

Feelers

Feelers avoid confrontation at all costs and are reluctant to disagree with people in a bid to avoid arguments. This is because they are mostly subjective and sympathetic when faced with problems; they often take things personally and can be overly emotional at times. They are constantly seeking approval from colleagues because they want to be liked and,in extreme cases, they can be perceived as bending over backwards to please people. Tender-hearted and always ready to compliment others, feelers value others and always focus on doing the right thing, considering their relationships and the impact of their actions on people around them. They are naturally interested in creating a collaborative environment, which in turn creates a sense of harmony and cooperation around them.

Working with feelers

Acknowledge their successes and be gentle in the way you criticize their work, because it is likely to impact their self-esteem. If you manage such people, it is important to provide them often with positive affirmation to boost their morale and confidence, which can have a direct impact on their performance.

How feelers can improve their relationship skills in the workplace

If you are a *feeler*, learn to understand that conflict, arguments and confrontation at work are not personal and try and work on managing your emotions to avoid being treated unfairly. Try to minimize your people-pleasing tendencies and learn to say 'no', because saying 'yes' all the time will lead to people taking advantage of your good nature.

Judging and perceiving

Judgers

Judgers like to make decisions in order to maintain structure and organization in their work and personal environments. They enjoy compiling and working to to-do lists and schedules to give them a better understanding about what is expected of them in each task that comes their way. They are not big fans of unpredictability and they hate surprises which can cause last-minute changes to their schedule. Completing a planned task according to its predetermined scope, time and cost gives judgers great pleasure and has a profound impact on their job satisfaction.

Working with judgers

Judgers are always plan-oriented and committed to having all their activities structured, so it is important to be respectful of their plans when interacting with them. Give them due credit for their ability to be organized and structured in pressured situations and try and understand that they might need some additional support in fast-paced, fast-changing environments.

How judgers can improve their relationship skills in the workplace

If you are a *judger*, remember that everything does not always work to plan and work on your flexibility. Try and be open to adapting your plan to accommodate sudden changes, and voice this out to your team members. Try being spontaneous sometimes and learn to understand that people around you will not be as structured and plan-oriented as you are.

Perceivers

Perceivers like the freedom attached to flexibility and prefer a work environment with few strict rules. They thrive on flexibility, welcome surprises and respond positively to urgent situations that require quick changes in predetermined plans. Having numerous options open to them is also important. Their attitude is based on a 'play now and work later' mentality and they enjoy the pressures that come with last-minute deadlines.

Working with perceivers

Acknowledge that they like being flexible and always remember to remind them about deadlines. Whenever you can, try not to be rigid with them, but emphasize the importance of committing to agreed deadlines in a gentle and subtle manner.

How perceivers can improve their relationship skills in the workplace

If you are a *perceiver*, avoid last-minute delays by developing your self-awareness skills to understand the expectations of people around you with regard to deadlines and commitments. Add some more structure to your work by creating a personal to-do list to regulate your workflow, which will help make you a little bit less spontaneous and allow your colleagues to be more at ease.

Conclusion

This chapter has attempted to explain the agile marketing mindset. Although it has not covered absolutely everything you need to know about personality types, it has provided a good overview of some of the key concepts that are relevant to marketing professionals. If you are interested in developing an agile marketing mindset, I would recommend that you research more about the topics included in this chapter to gain a better understanding about your personality type. This understanding can help you improve your self-awareness and social skills with colleagues and customers alike. This is necessary for marketing people and especially for customer-facing individuals who work in sales or B2B who are exposed to customer interaction on a daily basis. Understanding a customer's personality type when we interact with them can help us to manage and adapt our approach, thus reducing the risk of annoying or alienating customers and enabling us to create successful and long-lasting relationships between our organization and its core audiences and that – that makes all the difference.

We can all probably agree that the emotional welfare of the marketing team will impact their performance which will ultimately have a direct impact on the successful execution of marketing campaigns. A recent survey by the Australian Psychological Society revealed that 'nearly half of all working respondents (47%) reported workplace issues as a source of stress' and the World Health Organisation estimates that by the year 2020 'depression will be the second most debilitating condition in the developed world'. Work-related stress and office politics, therefore, have a direct impact on the quality of work, because employees can end up wasting a lot of valuable work time procrastinating due to lack of motivation.

A person's physical health is another important aspect of agility that a lot of us tend to ignore. In the UK and most everywhere else in the world, all cars are subject to regular MOT to inspect their roadworthiness in terms of carbon emissions and their overall safety on the road. How often do we check our own health MOT? By this I don't mean just focusing on healthy eating and working out. To be truly agile, we should make a point of scheduling a checkup at least once a year with a medical doctor who can evaluate the following metrics of our own personal agility:

» Blood Pressure

» Aerobic Fitness

» Heart Rate

» Total Cholesterol

» Blood Glucose

» Hydration

Chapter 3: Creating alignment in agile marketing

Creating a customer journey map

What is customer experience?

Customer experience is all about measuring and improving customer emotions. What comes to your mind when you think about your experience of shopping on Amazon, for example, or purchasing Apple products such as the iPhone and MacBook? As customers of these innovative brands, we get a feeling of trust and a consistent level of satisfaction across all the devices we use when interacting with them. According to Colin Shaw, author of the book *The Intuitive Customer,* 'A Customer Experience is a customer's perception of their rational, physical, emotional, subconscious, and psychological interaction with any part of an organisation. These perceptions influence customer behaviours and build memories, which drives customer loyalty and thereby affects the economic value an organisation generates.'

So why do we trust companies such as Amazon or Apple? From my personal perspective, I know that whatever product I purchase can be returned if I change my mind, and I am 100% certain that I will be refunded without any delays whatsoever. To manage the customer experience, a company has to develop trust with customers. Earning the trust of your customer depends on their perception of whether or not you are communicating false product benefits; customers need to know how reliable and competent you are as a business. Any inclusions or omissions within your marketing messages that might lead customers to believe that you took advantage of their lack of knowledge will negatively impact their experience with your brand. Customers are more interested in buying from brands that give them the impression that you have good intentions, rather than just being interested in taking their money. In other words, you want customers to enjoy doing business with you. Even when customers make mistakes with their purchase decisions, the very fact that some companies are determined to do what's right by the customer is what trust is about – adding that human touch. The best brands in the world are successful because customers know that the product or service they purchase from these companies will perform as expected – and if it doesn't, they are confident that they will get a full refund or replacement.

According to Don Peppers, author of the book *Customer Experience:* organizations must encourage all employees to see the business through the eyes of the customers. Marketing people have the responsibility to communicate the importance of customer experience to the rest of the organization, because a superior customer experience will have a direct impact on the revenue generated by the business. Customer information from CRM systems and web analytics provides marketers with reliable and sophisticated tool for ranking customers based on the revenue generated from them. After all, it's common knowledge that 80% of business profits most likely come from 20% of your customers. Later on in the chapter, we will discuss how marketing people can conduct regular interviews with customers in order to get feedback to understand customers' expectations and perceptions based on their interaction with a brand. A deeper understanding of your customers' interaction with your organization is needed to eliminate the friction points in their purchase journey and improve your customer loyalty. Therefore, organizations should move away from the mass-marketing approach and towards personalization, because every customer wants to be treated according to their individual requirements. For example, I enjoy customizing products I order online and this impacts my loyalty to brands that offer options of customization.

Today's customers expect a seamless experience with a business, both offline and online, but not many brands actually deliver this. These problems are sometimes due to the organizational silos where marketing does not communicate with IT, and where the offline stores have less communication with the web and digital marketing teams. Customers don't care about the internal structure of your organization – they just want a consistent experience across all channels and touchpoints. Fixing the internal structure of your organization to align with the omni-channel journey of your customers requires creating the right data, systems, analytics and other technologies to track, maintain and manage customer experience properly. In the next section, we will discuss how to create customer journey map next. This is a process that starts with gathering customer insights and continues through interviews, observations and social media insights to create profiles that then serve as input for the customer journey map creation process.

The customer interview as a starting point

Interviewing customers is the first step towards creating a customer journey map. To create a customer-focused marketing campaign, you must begin with a deep understanding of all your customer segments. It is easy to claim you already have such an understanding from web analytics data, but this represents just half of the insight you need to really understand your customers emotions and pain points. According to Jim Sterne, founder of eMetrics Summit & Digital Analytics Association, the qualitative insight you need to understand customers' perception and emotions is not possible with web analytics data. Marketing teams need to identify customers' feelings and perceptions about their brand and products through effective qualitative research. The context of qualitative research I am talking about is different from the A/B testing or user-testing widely employed in digital marketing teams. As marketing people, we are sometimes guilty of assuming we know what customers want, what they think, and what they like. We even go as far as rationalizing customer behaviour based on our personal experience.

When creating a customer experience strategy aimed at understanding and improving customer retention and loyalty, it is important to have full knowledge of your existing and new customers (customer on-boarding), ideally in the context of their individual purchase journeys and behaviours. The way to do this is to explore their behaviour, online through web analytics data, and complement this with the human qualitative insight obtained through person-to-person interviews and interactions with your customers. According to Jared Spool, marketing people should go to visit their customers in their homes, offices, or wherever they happen to be when they make the purchase of their product or service. Different segments of customer

Customer Interview

At the customer's home

should be interviewed in order to gather information about their experience when buying your product. Interviewing customers will help marketing teams to achieve the following:

> » Discover the behaviour and attitude of new and existing customers;

> » Provide opportunities to validate or nullify your assumptions about your customers;

> » Discover customers' frictions and emotional pain points with your product;

> » Discover the content-marketing needs of your customers.

The goal of customer interviews is to uncover customer frustrations and pain points with your website, email campaigns, mobile apps or in-store purchase experiences. These insights cannot be gained from web analytics; marketing teams need to dig for them through detailed customer observations. For example, your web analytics cannot tell you if your customers are having a bad experience with your sales team or your customer-service team, nor will web analytics tell you the reason why the customer expectations of your brand are changing. Interviews at different points within the customer buying process will identify new insights and opportunities that can be integrated into your website and content-marketing planning. Combining web analytics data with customer feedback from interviews will help capture actual customer behaviour that can then serve as an input for your customer retention and conversion optimization strategy. We have all been in situations where everyone in the marketing team seems to have a different interpretation of customer behaviour as generated from web analytics. Some might doubt the credibility of the data while others will argue about which channel should get the credit for customer conversion. Customer interviews create a shared experience from the perspective of the marketing team and from the knowledge gained about the experiences and emotions of the customer. These experiences allows senior stakeholders in the marketing team to develop empathy towards the customer because they reveal issues and paint points for the customer, which is not something that 'bounce-rate' metrics in web analytics can explain.

Richard Sheridan, CEO of Menlo Innovations, shared a story with me about one of his clients that hired his company to help market a diesel engine diagnostics tool (a yellow light on the motor's dashboard that alerts truck drivers about engine issues). The client wanted to create this new hand-held, touch-screen diesel engine diagnostics device. Richard's team was tasked with creating this new type of tool without any prior experience in this market, even though the client had over 30 years' experience in the industry.

Richard's team started with a visit to the local station to interview truck drivers. They requested an interview with a driver who was keen about the interview until he was told they were actually interested in observing him working. They told him: 'We want to see what you actually do, we want to hear you think out loud'. The team wanted to capture his vocabulary because what's important is to use the words that the customer uses. Too often in marketing we force our language onto customers. This is sometimes the case even with doctors; you go for a doctor's appointment and leave with the impression: 'Wow, the doctor seems really smart, even though I don't understand what he said, I am glad I have a smart doctor'. We should make it a point to observe customers working in their own environment, because some of the most important things marketing teams will discover about their customers are hidden in non-verbal clues; web analytics cannot report these types of insights.

Back to our story: while observing the truck driver at work, Richard's team noticed that he wore latex gloves before using any device, so they asked him why he did so. He responded that the gloves protects him from chemical substances that are known to be linked with the development of cancer. Remember that the client was asking Richard's team to design a device for touch screen, not pressure sensitive. Richard's team spent two hours interviewing the truck driver and returned to the office to ask their client: 'Did you know your customers wear latex gloves before using your device?' There was a dead silence: the client with over 30 years' experience in the industry didn't have a clue about their own customers' habits. Marketing teams often assume they know everything about their customers without ever meeting a customer face-to-face: how is that possible? No, you don't know your customers – you only know what Google tells you about your customers, which does *not* include their emotions. The customer research conducted by Richard's team resulted in a great success for the client and they currently dominate their industry precisely because of their new-found passion for customer research.

How to conduct customer interviews

In this section we will be discussing the practical experience of customer journey mapping with a range of examples from thought-leaders with extensive experience in agile marketing. Brian Raboin is currently the Vice President of Customer Experience at Booker Software, and he shared his experience of creating customer journey maps with me. According to him, the process starts with customer interviews that are used to develop personas which are then used as input for the customer journey map creation.

The first step is to gather everyone in the marketing team on-site in a meeting room, or over the phone for people who work remotely. The main objective of the meeting is to identify customer segments that each member of the team is interested in gathering qualitative insights about. It also involves creating a Task board with columns for everyone to update their pre-existing assumptions about customer behaviour, information needed, knowledge gaps, and the overall goal of the customer interview project. Steve Portigal in his book *Interviewing Users* suggested three key aspects of interviewing customers to be:

> » Making sure that questions used are all open-ended;

> » Asking customers to show you their purchase journey online rather than telling you what they did, which will allow you to observe actual behaviour;

» Asking them to tell you specific stories about their experiences with your brand, which will help you to gain insight about things you might not be able to observe while you are with them

Getting access to customers you wish to interview will depend on the objectives you are trying to achieve with the interview process. For existing customers, you can gather anywhere between 5 to 30 of them, in order to identify trends or patterns that will give you the necessary information to create a customer journey map. We must be aware that this number does not represent a statistically significant analysis; rather it is the qualitative insights that we are trying to gather. According to Portigal: 'trends are often observable from just five people'. As part of the customer interview process, the marketing team can obtain customer feedback from their colleagues in customer service and, most importantly, we can also research customer complaints on social-media platforms. Unsolicited customer feedback on social media is also a great source of information to identify the customer frictions we need to eliminate.

Monitoring social-media platforms such as Facebook, Twitter and Instagram for customer comments or mentions of your brand in either a positive or negative way will help you to establish the frictions and pain points that marketing can then communicate to the rest of the organization. Customers share their feelings and emotions freely with one another by talking about them on social-media platforms, and friends ask each other about their past experience with products. The more customer complaints marketing teams are able to discover online, the more information they can generate to create an insightful customer journey map.

Creating customer profiles is actually the output of the interview process – as opposed to the method of some marketing teams who create profiles of their customers based on assumptions off the top of their head while sitting at their desks, or through 'group brainstorming' sessions in the office. In the case of Brian Raboin's team at Booker Software, the customer interview is conducted in a collaborative manner by two members of the marketing team at the offices of their target customers. Representing a software company with B2B clients, Brian's team carry out the interviews at the actual location of the customer's office in order to observe them in their natural environment. The core principles of their approach to interviewing customers include:

1.   Making sure that they approach the interview with an open mind and the hunger to learn new information about their customer. It is better to be curious about the customer's perception, experience and opinion of their purchase journey with your brand as opposed to trying to conduct the interview process in ways that reaffirm your personal assumptions about your customer. Exclude all of your beliefs and hypotheses about your customers from the conversation and then enter a neutral space when interviewing the customer.

2.   Conducting interviews away from your offices - the objective of the process is to observe customers in their world, not yours. As marketing people, we sometimes feel we already know the answers to certain questions because of the web analytics and other quantitative data available to us. The truth of the matter is we do not have answers as to the 'why' behind the web analytics data; customer interview is the best way to learn more about the 'why' behind their purchase behaviour. When was the last time you looked your customers in the eyes to find out how and why they interact with your website in certain ways?

3.   Probing the customer for information while observing their body language at the same time. Ask your customers open-ended questions such as: 'tell me the process you went through the last time you purchased something online through your smartphone' and make sure to maintain eye contact with them while asking follow-up questions as the conversation develops.

According to Brian, one of the key challenges in conducting customer interviews is the selection of the sample of customers to be included in the process of developing customer personas. How should marketing people select customers to interview? Should we interview the highest-paying customers, new customers (customer on-boarding), or churning customers? From a strategic perspective, marketing must decide which customer segment they want to target, interview the relevant customers, and create a customer journey map that serves as input into the agile process and task board. Look at the customer segments you already have, identify who these customers are, and find out more about their background. Ask those customers what they like and don't like about your product or service. Also, ask customers what problems they experience with your product or service and try to figure out a way to solve these, in order to retain these customers for the long term. You can ask direct questions such as :

> » What do you like about our product/service?

> » What do we do well?

> » Why do you choose us?

> » What did we end up not doing well that has annoyed you? (We can then go and fix it.)

Focusing on these things is important to maintain customer retention, which ultimately facilitates the organic growth of a business. Identifying why customers like your product and portraying that as your distinctive competency can be really useful in creating marketing campaigns that increase sales.

Creating a customer or buyer profile

Before creating customer persona profiles, you also need to understand the goals of each customer and the reasons why they purchase from you instead of your competitors. Profiles help you to identify your customers, understand their buying decision processes and their perception about your product in comparison with that of your competitors, as well as identify what part of your value proposition they find appealing. What is the profile of your new customers (customer on-boarding), existing customers, and customers that have defaulted to your competitors? What is the profile of people that are loyal to your competitors? For those organisations that do not currently have an existing profile of their customer base, it is important to research and create as soon as possible. If you don't know who your customers are, then you don't have a clear picture of what they want and what their pain points are, or what makes them happy about your product and what problems or needs your product solves. By creating a profile representation of your customer types, you are able to identify and understand customers' positive and negative emotions for your brand from the first time they interact with it and all the way through their journey to discover whether repeat purchase and continuous engagement occur with your brand.

Creating a customer profile will identify the main motivation of your customers. However, be mindful how you go about this: arriving at assumptions about your customer profile from internal stakeholders is not the recommended way to do it, even though this is the most common method that companies will use. Creating marketing strategies around assumed profiles is a recipe for a waste of marketing budget through targeting the wrong customers and channels. Go outside and try to find your typical customer at large – don't just rely on web analytics data alone. You will be able to better understand which marketing channel, device and communication method would appeal to these customers to generate sales.

After researching everything you know about your customers, group them into a profile template - you can download a blank customer persona template online and fill in the information you gather from your customer interviews. It's important to understand that creating a profile is an iterative process and not just a one-off event. Creating customers' or buyers' persona profiles starts by talking face-to-face with the actual customers and combining this with actively listening to customers on social-media channels such as Facebook, Twitter, LinkedIn and others. If you have physical store locations (bricks-and-mortar retail companies), it's important to observe customer purchases from your sotres in real life and to interview customers, in person or remotely, to gain a rich source of contextual insights that are not available in the raw data provided by web analytics platforms. Come up with a name and photo for your profile to be able to differentiate and identify your typical customer and make him or her more lifelike to your team.

Components of a customer profile

A standard customer profile will contain the following five components:

A name

A photo

Brief description of the profile with an emphasis on their goals

Challenges

Emotions

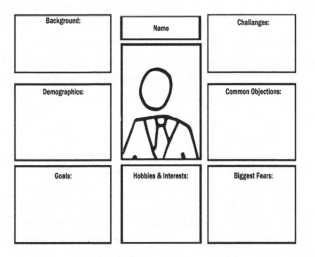

An example of a customer profile

According to Brian Raboin, marketing people often tend to develop imaginary customer profiles that are based on what they think their customers should be; they seem to forget that there are real, living customers they can talk to in order to develop accurate customer profiles. The work marketing teams do in preparation for the journey-mapping is crucial for understanding their customers. To create customer profiles, Brian's team started with a pre-interview questionnaire. There are about eight people in his team, who split into four pairs and went out to meet the customers and spend a day with them. They met these customers in their own environment, observed how they used the company's products (software) and interviewed them. Then the interview team came back to the office and brainstormed to develop the customer profiles of the people who use these software products. These profiles, then, are based on their observations of real people using Booker Software products – they're not just conjured up from the limited and scattered information usually available to marketing people.

It is really important to share the profiles you create across your marketing teams and the entire organization in order to encourage a shared understanding of your target customers. Also, remember that the best profile from which you can get a wealth of relevant insights is that of the customers that buy from your competitors; these are the people that didn't buy from you but decided to buy from competitors - something contributed to this decision and you need to know what that was, if you are going to be able to compete.

What is a customer journey map?

During my conversation with Brian, he told me that, in his experience, finding a problem worth solving is the precursor to agile. If you are trying to put together great ideas, you can never be sure that there is a market out there. Finding customers that you want to serve and then mapping what their experience is – this is where a customer journey map comes in. Agile is not the first stage of building whatever you are trying to achieve for your company. An important stage that needs to precede agile is figuring out what the problems are in the first place. This can be done by mapping out your existing customers' journey map, whether you are trying to increase sales of existing products and services or push new products. Creating a shared goal across the marketing team helps to break down silos within the organisation by creating alignment with the intention of creating happy customers. It also helps marketing teams to create maps for each profile and to target campaign activities at each segment, for example, the team at Booker Software created journey maps for existing customers, new customers (customer on-boarding), and premium customers.

Agile marketing also works well with start-ups. As a start-up, you can look at existing companies in the industry you want to compete in and identify key aspects you believe to be 'broken' or missing. You can then begin to create a journey map of the current customer experience to discover what you will need to focus on to compete successfully within that industry. For example, start-ups could say: 'Let us create a journey map to find out what it's like to try to travel from London to New York for a weekend during an Apple product release or for a conference such as Oracle OpenWorld or even for a music concert'. Journey maps are created largely from data gathered through customer interviews. As an existing business, you can fairly easily develop a customer journey map because you can just dig into your customer relationship management systems to gather relevant customer information. Just call up your customers and talk to them, invite them over to your office, or visit them at work (or at home, if it's appropriate), and interview them to understand their buying behaviour.

Customers always remember their experiences with your brand, whether good, bad or indifferent. The primary objective of the marketing team in every organization is to make sure that its customers have a good experience before, during and after they complete the purchase of a product or service. Do you know all of the touchpoints that your customers are going through to be able to buy your product? We sometimes believe that all this information is available in web analytics, but that is only half of the picture, because web analytics cannot analyse customer emotions or motivations to buy. The other half relates to your customers perception of your brand in their specific purchasing context and this is formed through their interactions with your brand, i.e. their overall journey (Offline and online).

We have discussed the process of interviewing customers and creating profiles from the interview process; the output of these activities contributes to the creation of the journey map. A customer journey map is the end-to-end visualization of all the touch-point interactions customers have with an organization from pre-purchase to after-sales experiences. It serves as a source of insight that helps marketing teams to understand customers better because it visually illustrates the customer-purchase process, and their needs and perceptions of your brand at different touch points. Customer journey maps help marketing teams to understand the existing purchase behaviour of customers with a particular emphasis on their emotional experience, frictions and pain points they experience in their purchase path. This insight identifies which points in the buying journey or product life cycle are below customer's expectations and this informs business decisions on where and how to improve the product or service offerings. However, what about the marketing insight blind spots? I'm sure we can all agree that not all customer journeys start from a company website or Google search and that there are some touch points that are not always explicitly visible within the customer journey map. One type of these invisible touch points, for example, are interactions of your customers with their friends and family to seek their feelings and opinions about previous experiences with your brand. The only way to learn about these invisible touch points in the customer journey is to observe customers and interview them, as we discussed earlier in this chapter.

It is important to understand what customers are going through in order to access what they want from your organization; this interaction also happens after they have completed a purchase – something else that is not always captured in web analytics. Touch-point mapping is important in terms of explaining the context of the customer-purchase process. Understanding the perception of customers towards your organization helps to highlight weaknesses and inefficiencies in your overall marketing and customer communications strategy. Creating a customer journey map should be a group activity that involves

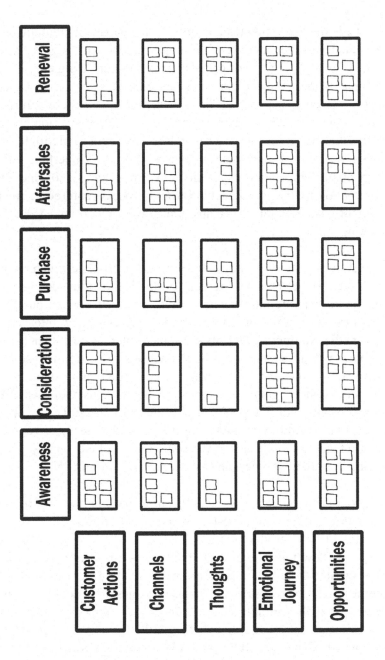

An example of a customer journey map

everyone in the marketing team in order to foster a team mentality and an acceptance of the outcome of the mapping process. Insights gained from customer journey maps can also help non-marketing employees and other internal stakeholders to develop an understanding of and empathy towards customers. This, then, helps to generate further insights and strategies to achieve overall customer satisfaction, which directly impacts on business revenue. It is important to highlight that brands have control over their customers' journeys in certain paths, but no control in others, especially those that happen offline. We now move on to discuss the activities and process required to create intelligent customer journey maps and how to keep them fresh for marketing agility.

The customer journey is not always a linear process, much as we would like it to be. The main reason for this is the influence of social media and other external influences that impact customers' purchase behaviours. The information gathered from customer interviews, social-media comments, and insights from internal customer-facing employees will all be important when creating an insightful customer journey map. Too many organizations base their understanding of customers on their personal opinions and perceptions about what the customer wants. For companies that want to have a full view about their customers from a qualitative and quantitative perspective, their marketing teams should rely on the combination of customer journey mapping and web analytics data as a complementary insights.

The set of journeys and paths customers pass through from awareness, consideration, purchasing, post-purchase and becoming loyal brand advocates of your product can be developed into a single customer journey to show the overall customer life cycle. Journey maps can also be created to show the purchase phase alone, for customers who enter the purchase process at non-standard stages of the journey. These experiences span multiple channels and touchpoints that ultimately affect the perception, trust and credibility of your organization. Customers don't care about the internal structure of your organization; they see customer service, online platforms and your physical store as a single experience – and they want a seamless and consistent level of service across all their interactions with your organisation.

Customer journey maps help to align the internal structure of the organization to highlight friction points that are causing stress to customers. Customer retention can then be improved by reducing this emotional stress; a good customer interaction encourages repeat purchases and recommendations to others customers through word of mouth. It also helps marketing teams to provide customer pain-point information to other departments within the organization with a view as to how they can improve their service, which in turn solves broader problems relating to overall business processes. Web analytics data cannot provide all the answers to business problems, especially to issues relating to the decline in revenue due to the arrival of new competitors, existing customer churns, and fewer sales due to external factors. Customer journey maps help to identify the reasons for revenue decline and other issues that can only be uncovered through close observation of customer behaviour.

The process of creating a customer journey map involves collaboration between multiple stakeholders from marketing, IT, sales, customer services and other client-facing employees in the organization. Assembling these individuals together to create an end-to-end customer journey map facilitates a culture of alignment across the organization because satisfying customers is a shared objective across all departments in the organization. It also enables customer-focused decision making, which helps organizations and marketing teams to shift from making assumptions about customer behaviour to actually collecting qualitative insights to inform strategic decisions. Marketing campaigns are often structured around product features but the focus can be changed towards a customer-problem focus through insights gained from customer journey maps.

How to create a customer journey map?

The process of creating a customer journey map starts with the identification of customer segments, which result from the profiles developed through the interviewing process, existing research by customer-service teams, information from call logs and various other sources. It also requires the use of tools such as digital whiteboards, online mapping tools and physical whiteboards in a 'war room'. Common elements of customer journey maps are:

» Profiles

» Scenarios (goals, or tasks that customer is trying to accomplish)

» Journey phases

» Channels

» Devices

» Emotions

» Insights

Profiles

Profiles should not be figments of your imagination, which they would be if you were to sit in your office and create a profile of your ideal customer without actually talking to customers in the real world. Marketing people create profiles as a representation of customer segments as a response to information gleaned from observing and interviewing customers. These profiles could represent new customers (customer on-boarding), existing customers, or loyal advocates of your product or service, or any other segment specific to your product or service.

Scenarios

The purchase process with the goal of in store 'Click and collect' is an example of a typical scenario. Another example is when customers contact product support for installation or repairs. We have already discussed how qualitative insights about our customers can be obtained by focusing on the friction points, delays and inconsistencies of product messaging the customer endures. The marketing team can use these to develop strategies which will help the brand to improve the overall customer experience. This is where marketing aligns itself with the other parts of the organization that customers interact with in order to improve customer experience, because marketing does not have direct influence over all the stages of a customer's interaction with the brand.

Journey phases

Journey phases are the stages the customer goes through; they should be structured from the customer's perspective – and not the marketing team's perspective. Examining these phases creates a better understanding of customer emotions, devices and triggers at each stage, which directly impacts their overall experience. Grouping together similar and meaningful types of customer behaviour into defined stages provides a better way of gaining valuable customer insights. The customer purchase journey phases fall under the following categories:

- » Product awareness;

- » Research;

- » Consideration, evaluation and comparison;

- » Purchase decision;

- » Retention (post-purchase stage);

- » Advocacy (post-purchase stage).

Channels

A channel denotes the space in which the interaction between your organization and customer takes place. Technology has increased the number of channels through which customers are able to complete their purchase journey. While some channels are more convenient than others, the customer journey map helps marketing teams to understand why customers switch between channels, and which channels are potentially causing stress for customers. Why does a customer start their purchase journey on your app, switch to your website, and then decide to order over the phone? Interviewing such customers would help marketing teams to learn where and how to optimize the overall omni-channel customer experience from online, in store, mobile text, and across a range of other channels. According to Nielsen Norman Group, there are five important components for creating a successful omni-channel customer experience: consistency, seamlessness, optimization, orchestration, and collaboration.

Emotions

According to recent research by Forrester, emotions are the most important influence on customer loyalty. Emotions are the strongest driver of customer retention and advocacy. The research also showed that customers' emotions had a direct impact on brands' online reputations, because delighted customers will definitely share their positive experience, whereas angry customers will spread negative comments about their experience with friends and family. Customers experience different types of emotions through their purchase journey and overall interaction with your company. At some points they find the experience easy and seamless, whilst at other points they encounter difficulties and frictions, which impacts their motivation either to continue the purchase journey or to leave. The emotional 'highs' and 'lows' of customers are visualized in this section of the journey map. Identifying these emotions helps marketing teams to understand the pleasure or pain the customer is experiencing as they interact with the organization.

The emotional reactions of customers can cause them to switch from online purchase to offline, and sometimes to cancel the complete purchase through calling customer services, or just relying on your app. The switch between devices and touch points can be captured by web analytics but it still misses the emotional element, which is one of the reasons behind customer churns. The moment your customers realize that your competitors offer a better experience, they will switch – regardless of any price differential. Emotions influence future purchase decisions as well as current ones. Even though emotions have been identified as the number-one driver of customer retention and loyalty, companies continue to ignore their customers' emotions because they don't possess the necessary skills for customer journey mapping. Another excuse for companies failing to measure their customers' emotions can be linked to the perception that 'if you can't measure it, you can't manage it' – which is why some companies are going bankrupt.

Devices

Different devices provide different functionalities and purchase experiences to customers because the screen size and input capabilities for information vary between devices. This is one of the key areas where customer journey maps can be really useful: providing important insights and understanding about customer transition between devices and the friction points that could be addressed to encourage a seamless transition between devices.

Customers use different devices in different locations; it's important for marketing teams to understand the experiences of customers as they switch between devices. As customers ourselves, we sometimes start researching on the desktop at work, continue on the mobile phone on the train home, and switch to a tablet at home. The seamless transition between the use of all these devices, without the stress of log-in and log-out, or starting the journey over and over again, is very important for customer experience. Observing and interviewing customers to ascertain the reasons behind their converting to a particular device will allow marketing teams to tailor their advertising and content-marketing strategies to fit the device. Of course, some devices are being used in different channels, for example, mobile phones can be used to order online as well as in store to review product information.

Insights

Insights are the key to customer experience improvement opportunities and to areas where friction and pain points for the customer can be addressed. The insights section of a customer journey map contains all the revelations about customers' emotions, channels, devices, and journey phases for any specific customer segment. These insights serve as input for the agile marketing team and other departments because they help to prioritize tasks and indicate where the organization should focus its resources in order to improve the overall omni-channel customer experience. The insights arising from the customer journey map are important for creating the implementation plan that feeds into the agile marketing plan.

The end-to-end customer journey, from the point when the customer first hears about your organization, through to their first purchase, and right the way through to when they become a loyal customer, provides a journey map of a customer's lifetime with your organization. The insight gained is key for the alignment of different departments in an organization because everyone is then able to see how the customer interacts with different departments through their journey, so that these teams can start collaborating to improve the overall customer journey.

Understanding which customer segment to journey map

Whether you are journey-mapping your existing customers or new customers, the process is similar. When marketing teams create a journey map of a brand-new customer, it is better to start with real, existing customers who have gone through the purchase process of your existing product or service. This is the type of customer you want, so you map what really happened to them and document the facts of their journey from their point of view. For B2B customers, you visit them in their office and explore how they started the research of your product or service; with their permission, look at the email exchanges and phone calls they had with your company as they journeyed towards purchasing your product. Doing this with a handful of customers will lead to a better understanding of the broader profile base of your customers, which helps you develop a profile-based journey map. This is an interesting process because it also tells you how disciplined you are with your own internal procedures. You might say: 'Hey, I have these three customers and these are the types of customer I want and I expect them all to follow the same journey'. But if these customers don't follow the same journey as you expected, then you've identified a problem: a weakness in getting customers through your organization. This would then be a good place to start working on how to fix your organizational structure to meet your customer flow.

In a B2B context, an additional complication arises when you have more than one person making the decision. A customer journey in B2B is still very much people-to-people, which means that somebody inside one business is going to be working with somebody inside the other business. You usually have a single point of contact, or you might get re-routed to another point of contact, and the journey map might change as some people might come into the purchase-decision process while some people might fall off it. However, the whole journey necessarily does not change because it is still about one person dealing with a system's group of people.

So what are the benefits of a journey map and how do you action the insights resulting from its creation? A journey map helps you to identify steps that matter to the customer in their experience of the journey within your organization. Your marketing team must be able to understand which things your customers consider to be your core strengths, which you can then capitalize and improve upon. The map can also help you to identify where the customer journey fails and where the customer experience is bad; this can help your marketing team to develop different ways to improve. Customer journey maps can also reveal problems that customers face in general, which can then lead to new product development, breaking into new business segments, or introducing new features for existing products. An analysis of the whole customer journey map leads to three key revelations:

1.   Where we can capitalize;

2.   Where we are weak in our current internal process;

3.   Where there are brand-new opportunities that we could explore.

When you have identified these three areas, you can incorporate them into the business and relay this information to all the internal departments affected by customer experience.

Conclusion

Marketing is the responsibility of everyone within the organisation, from Customer Service, Sales, Human Resources, Aftersales and other support teams. This is why it is important for marketing teams to effectively collaborate with other departments within the business to create a seamless end-to-end customer journey. Customer journey maps, therefore, serve as a tool for alignment which highlights dependencies between teams and individuals and how their performance in their role helps improve the overall customer experience. They also help create a shared vision because they make every employee aware of the customer's perspective. The HR, Sales and customer services teams can then create their own journey maps to generate insights that lead to action on how to improve the experiences of both internal and external customers.

Chapter 4: How to Become Agile in Marketing

Pre-implementation requirements for agile marketing

According to Sean Zinsmeister, Vice President Product Marketing at Infer.com, an agile marketing team must have a shared goal and vision when creating a marketing plan. Every member of the team *must* have access to the integrated marketing plan. Planning and forecasting of customer acquisition, engagement, conversion and retention metrics is a daunting task, which is made more difficult by the expanding number of customer touchpoints and interactions. The insights generated from customer journey maps provide crucial input for marketing strategy and facilitate the prioritization of tasks to be completed by each member of the agile marketing team. Team members are also encouraged to continuously update their contribution to the marketing plans on a regular basis, as and when new customer insight is discovered.

We frequently fail to acknowledge that we are prone to creating marketing plans based on assumptions alone, without integrating valid insights from web analytics or considering any relevant qualitative insights (such as customer emotions). In chapter 3 we discussed the importance of creating competitors' customer journey maps to acquire new knowledge not just about your competitors, but also about your customers. This can help significantly enhance the accuracy of our planning and execution of marketing tactics to improve campaign success. The first step, however, should always focus on understanding your current situation and this is done through a detailed situation analysis.

Situation analysis

In order to create an effective marketing plan, organizations must first understand the situation of its internal (employees, resources and technology) and external (competitors and macro elements) environment. Through conducting a situation analysis, marketing people access and collect information about the current state of their marketing team, strategy, tools and external environment. This allows them to understand the factors that influence customer acquisition, engagement, retention and overall customer experience. This also serves as a reality check against business objectives agreed with the CEO or the Board of Directors, in the case of publicly trading companies.

Marketing people often ask themselves: where, how and what do I need to conduct a situation analysis of my organization's marketing capability? The answer is easy because marketing technology tools, such as web analytics and other customer-listening tools, offer a rich source of data to evaluate the current situation of your marketing activities. The only potential drawbacks can be the flawed inter-pretation of metrics in web analytics as well as an over-reliance on quantitative customer insights to the detriment of qualitative insights. Customers have evolved from the pre-Internet one-way marketing communication models that allowed companies to spread information without means of verification by consumers. In a previous chapter we discussed the importance of customer interviews towards creating a live customer journey map that is consistently updated every six weeks to keep abreast of changing customer expectations and perceptions. This is why situation analysis is no longer a luxury, but a necessity, if companies want to survive and improve the ROI of their marketing activities. Listening to customers through customer journey maps is the best way to conduct situation analysis because these will reveal information about which part of your offering appeals to customers or irritates them, as well as useful information about your competitors.

Situation analysis should also include an audit of the internal recruitment process of the team because if marketing teams fail to monitor the type of people entering the team, the culture could become toxic and this will have a strong negative impact on campaign performance. In the famous words of Peter Drucker: 'Culture eats strategy for breakfast' - every time! To learn more about the impact of HR practices on agile marketing, please refer to the case study section of this book where I have included a case study about the agile marketing team at Bookers Software who work with the HR team to recruit and develop agile marketing teams.

PESTLE analysis

A big part of the situation analysis comes down to understanding the external macro environment in which the business operates. The most useful marketing tool to do this is the PESTLE analysis, which evaluates political, economic, social–cultural, technological, legal and environmental factors within the external environment. Creating and implementing marketing plans needs to be heavily informed by these factors to avoid any serious business, legal or political issues that could negatively impact on the organization.

For multinational organizations, it is important to understand the political situation that exists in countries like China and Russia, in comparison to that in the USA, because government policies in different countries can seriously affect how you market your product and services in these countries. As a marketing professional, are you aware how much cultural differences and technological innovations affect your strategy? Can you implement a single strategy across all regions or do you need to create bespoke marketing strategies for different regions? For example, legislation in Russia requires multinational companies to store information about Russians within its borders, which has resulted in the blacklisting of companies that failed to comply with this requirement.

From a strategic perspective, it is vital to understand every part of the PESTLE framework when creating, reviewing and updating marketing plans. Let's look at each element of the PESTLE analysis to see how it should be considered in the context of agile marketing.

Political

How does the political relationship between your home country and other countries affect the new markets your organization is trying to enter? The political factors determine the extent to which you are able to expand your offshore marketing teams, so it frames your consideration of whether or not you should consider hiring contractors as part of your marketing teams in order to deliver your product or service in unstable regions. What are the tax policies in these countries like and how does that affect your pricing, as well as logistics, throughout the region from a strategic planning perspective?

Economic

These factors determine the economic performance that influences your marketing plan because of its impact on customers' purchasing power.

Social-Cultural

Consumers today are increasingly aware and vocal about social issues. Corporate social responsibility affects the consumer perception of a brand and contributes to its aura of integrity and trustworthiness. A good example for this context is the reaction of consumers to brands associated with the current US President, Donald Trump. Due to his unconventional behavior and opinions, which many find offensive, consumers are beginning to distance themselves from brands that appear to support or endorse President Trump and this has nothing to do with price of customer experience. These consumers do not want their purchase decisions or their money to benefit Donald Trump in any way, shape or form. This is also slowly impacting the businesses of other companies owned and managed by other members of the Trump family, as well as their extended business networks

Technological

What technological tools are you currently using for your marketing initiatives and how does that impact the overall customer experience of your brand? Do the technological tools at your disposal provide a seamless and effortless experience for customers, or are they telling different stories or, perhaps, creating difficulty for customers to access the information they require? It is important to constantly review new marketing tools with an emphasis on how relevant they are to your specific marketing objectives and your target audiences, as well as whether or not they help improve customer satisfaction.

Legal

In every market there will exist both external and internal legislation that will impact customer information in relation to how marketing teams can store or share information without customers' consent. Most countries around the world will have some form of legislation to protect personal identifiable information. These can be particularly stringent in the USA and Europe and marketing teams are expected to comply with any such legislation when planning and implementing their marketing strategies.

Environmental

Retail and e-commerce companies in the clothing industry are not the only ones that need to pay attention to climate conditions to determine what product to sell in different climates around the world. Consumers in almost every industry are increasingly worried about the impact of the business production processes on the environment. They worry about what products are created and how (ethical sourcing), as well as how that impacts on global warming. The automobile industry's carbon footprint and its overall impact on the environment, for example, create a competitive advantage for electric and solar-powered car manufacturers like Tesla.

Customer analysis

As marketing people, whenever we think about our customers, we often ask ourselves three questions about their profile:

1.   Who is my ideal customer?

2.   Why does my customer buy from me and not from my direct or indirect competitors?

3.   How do my customers buy from me and which channels do they use?

We look at each of these questions in greater detail in the following sections.

Your ideal customer

Understanding who your customer is requires getting out of the building and interviewing people who buy your products, as well as those who decided not to purchase from you and chose to go elsewhere. Web analytics and other qualitative insights within your organization will not reveal the emotional states of your customers. You need to interview and observe customers to be able to develop a customer profile and we discuss how to create a customer profile in the next section of this chapter.

As marketers, we sometimes make assumptions about who the target customer is based on our internal company logic and our perception of an ideal customer. This is perfectly understandable: you will always consider first the information that is (relatively) easy to obtain. However, assumptions based on this type of information can lead to an extreme waste of marketing funds on strategies that are completely irrelevant to our prospective customers. This is why it is essential to know the exact profile of your customers. The focus, in particular, needs to be on new customers, existing customers (both those that are high-purchasers and those that arc low-purchasers), and creating opportunities to develop and sustain loyalty in both of these types of customers. In order to define these opportunities, you will also need to develop profiles for your competitors' customers, in order to understand customer experience issues that might make customers switch loyalty from your company to your competitors, as well as vice versa.

Your customers' reasons for buying from you (and not your competitors)

There are many factors that influence why customers choose to purchase a product from your company as opposed to buying from your competitors. In chapter 3, we discussed the importance of customer research to create personas as input into the customer journey mapping process. To understand the reason why, Dr Flint McGlaughlin, the founder and Managing Director of MECLABS, and a world renowned expert on conversion optimisation, argues that customers buy from you based on the clarity of the value your product provides in combination with how your communication with them reduces their anxiety while increasing their motivation to buy your product, playing up the perceived benefits that your product provides. Below is McGlaughlin's formula that explains why your customers buy from you:

$$C = 4M + 3V + 2 (I - F) - 2A$$

Wherein:

C = Probability to purchase

M = Motivation to buy (when)

V = Clarity of value proposition (why)

I = Incentive to take purchase action

F = Friction elements in buying process

A = Anxiety about trusting and engaging with your company

Probability to purchase

To be able to understand why customers buy from you, it is necessary to research which features of your product customers find particularly appealing and whether or not they believe these features are exclusive to your brand. In other words, do they think your product is different and more appealing than that of your competitors? Factor this into your communication with customers through your online and offline marketing channels so that customers have the information they need to make a purchase decision. McGlaughlin has also highlighted that, in order for your product offering to be appealing to customers, it needs to be relevant to the need the customer is trying to fulfil by purchasing your product. The exclusivity part of your product can be pitched as there being very few alternatives to your product on the market. The perceived value of your product increases if customers believe that your competitors' alternative lacks the same features as those present in your product which they find important.

Motivation to buy

What motivates your customer to purchase? What problems are they trying to solve and how do your marketing campaigns communicate how your product or service is able to solve their problems? It is the role of marketing to portray the product value from a problem-solving perspective, rather than from a feature-related communication to customers and this increases customers' motivation to buy your product. The higher the existing motivation of your customers when they come into contact with your product, the easier it will be for them to make a purchase. Customers are motivated by the benefits your product offers and by the trust and credibility they perceive in your product. For your existing customers these are based on their previous use of your product and for your new customers these are based on the impact of your marketing campaign, or possibly word of mouth from friends, family, comparison and review websites, or similar channels.

Clarity of value proposition

Customers will simply ask: why should I buy your product? What's in it for me? You need to emphasize what value your customers will derive from buying and using your product by clearly explaining how your product serves their needs. What is the value proposition of your product and how clearly is it communicated to your customers as it relates to their needs? Customers are also curious about your competence in terms of product quality. How can you communicate to your customers that your product is of the highest quality and meets their demands? This is the type of communication necessary to convince your customers to buy your product.

Incentive to take purchase action

For some products customers are easily motivated to buy based on how competitive your pricing is. You can offer additional incentives to the core-value proposition, such as time-limited discounts or bonuses if the action is taken (e.g. buy one, get one free). The communication of such incentives to potential buyers gives them an additional reason to purchase, making their motivation even stronger.

Friction elements in the buying process

According to Forrester Research, one of the most influential research and advisory companies in the world, customer experience is the new battleground for brands that want to succeed in the 'age of the customer'. The number of frictions and pain points that customers experience when interacting with your brand through various channels and touchpoints will determine whether they purchase from you or from your competitors. How many friction elements exist in your purchase and post-purchase journey? For example, the number of fields in the form to fill in, or in the case of a multi-step process, the stages required to register on your website are obvious friction elements. Reducing friction in your customer purchase and post-purchase experience will give potential customers another reason to choose your product over that of your competitors.

Anxiety about trusting and engaging with your company

We sometimes over-emphasize the retail capability and website advancement of Amazon, but in reality the most important reason why people buy from Amazon is the trust they have for the brand. Customers are not afraid to make a purchase on Amazon because they have no anxiety about getting a refund if the product does not meet their expectations and this lack of anxiety is based on extreme trust in the brand. The same can be said about Apple: customers trust Apple to create and maintain quality computer and mobile phone products because of its organizational credibility and corporate values. Aside from corporate or brand credentials, another big aspect of trust is data protection. Customers experience copious amounts of anxiety arising from the fear regarding the level of privacy and security of their personal data once they enter it on your website. It is therefore important to reassure your website visitors through clear communication about how and when their data is likely to be used, giving them the option to opt in or out of certain features or activities.

Your customers' buying patterns and preferred channels

A thorough situational analysis would require an in-depth audit of your customers' purchase journeys to determine the channels and touchpoints that are most effective to reach your new and existing customers. You will need to consider what keywords they search for on Google when looking for the types of product you sell, as well as what types of content they research in the evaluation phase, before the final purchasing decision is made. Another thing to consider are also the content requirements and customer experience needed to retain customers for repeat purchases and keep them loyal to your brand.

Competitor analysis

There is a popular saying that says 'Keep your friends close and your enemies closer', which is very relevant to competitor analysis in marketing. You definitely want to understand the strengths and weaknesses of your organization in comparison to your direct and indirect competitors and to be able to analyse and benchmark your marketing strategy against that of your competitors, you must first identify who they are. What share of the total customer base of your industry is being controlled by your competitors and how loyal are your potential customers to your competitor? How different are your competitors' value propositions and how serious are they in terms of team structure, skills and overall execution of their customer experience initiatives?

A while ago, whilst negotiating the prospect of consulting for a well-known charity in the UK, I asked them to tell me about their competitors and they replied that they didn't really have any competitors, apart from their corporate partner's charity foundation. I then asked them why they didn't consider other charities as competitors and the reply was that other charities didn't address the same issue they did, so they weren't regarded as competitors. This is a typical example of a flawed way in which some marketing teams view competitors - just because an organization does not deliver exactly the same product or service as you do, that does not mean that they should be discounted as a competitor. At the end of the day, you are competing for a proportion of a customer's disposable income, which is limited. Therefore, you should take a broader view of the competition and make sure you are crafting an appealing message about an unbeatable set of benefits and that you are delivering this message through the channels your customers use most frequently.

Another common error when defining competitors is made when marketing teams rely heavily on Google search to understand who they are competing against. What if those competitors are not very active online - does that mean that they should not be researched or considered? Of course not, as a marketing professional it is your job to follow where the research takes you, regardless of whether that's in the digital or the physical space.

So how do we research competitors and what questions should we be asking in order to gather intelligence that will be useful and actionable within the agile marketing decision-making process? In my experience of consulting for large and medium-sized marketing teams, coupled with the insights I gained from conversations with marketing thought-leaders, potential and existing customers are the best medium for acquiring such knowledge. Sitting down and having a face-to-face conversation with your potential, existing and, most importantly, your competitors' customers will provide you with all the necessary information about your competitors' strengths and weaknesses. It is also important - and relatively easy - to research your competitors' websites, social-media platforms, as well as paid and organic search advertising strategy and rankings. Somewhat more difficult will be to discover their team structure and capabilities in terms of marketing technology, but if you are persistent and resourceful, this also is not an insurmountable issue.

Porter's Five Forces

Another useful tool to understanding where your product or service (or organization) fits within the industry is the Porter's Five Forces framework. Devised in 1979 by Professor Michael Porter, it represents a framework to analyse the competitive nature of an industry in terms of profitability and attractiveness. You might wonder how this model is relevant to agile marketing. The short answer is that revenue and profits generated from your marketing strategy will be determined by the competitive structure of the market you operate in. Although you are competing with your direct competitors that produce similar products or services, it is important to also look at your indirect competitors, i.e. the companies that produce alternative products to those you are trying to market to your consumers, because you are all competing for the consumer's limited disposable income.

Most marketing professionalas believe that competition is won by creating a product with better features and pricing strategy than that of their direct competitors. Our experience of marketing in the 'age of the consumer', however, demonstrates that consumers of today have an ingrained expectation of receiving high-quality products at reasonable prices, and this is a sort of 'baseline' requirement, rather than a viable strategy for differentiation. Value is now created through providing *better* customer experience to your target audience than your competitors offer. Therefore, the real point of researching your competitors is not just about acquiring more customers than them, but about winning over your competitors' existing customers, whilst retaining your own customer base and the only way to do this successfully is by providing an outstanding customer experience. Successful competition for customers' attention and loyalty is the only way to guarantee increased and sustainable business revenue and should be at the heart of every marketing activity,.

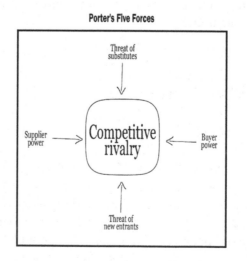

Porter's Five Forces

As part of competitor research, it is important to interview customers about products and services that they consider as alternatives to yours. You need to understand, from the perspective of your customers, which products or services might satisfy the same needs as your product does, albeit in a different way. An accounting firm might view other accounting companies as competitors, but would they view account software packages such as Sage and QuickBooks as their competitors too? Researching indirect competitors is difficult because they often come from unexpected industries. Apple and Netflix, for example, were not direct competitors to CD manufacturing and movie rental companies until a shift in technology resulted in consumer behaviour changing in favour of video streaming. This, as well all know, led to the collapse of big high-street brands in recent years.

Whatever the industry your business operates in, there will always be newcomers seeking a share of the market, because improvement in technological infrastructure has reduced the barriers to entry for most industries. The threat of new competitors is real and present; the emergence of companies such as Airbnb and Uber is a good example of how new, indirect competitors can not only compete for your customers but can also run you out of business. The only way to stay ahead of the game is to constantly review your competitive landscape, identify new potential competitors early enough and make adjustments to your marketing strategy to be able to keep your advantage whilst they are entering into the market. Ultimately, the onus is on you to size up the threat of new competitors entering the market, evaluate to role of your existing competitors and adjust your marketing strategy accordingly. I present some possible ways to do this in the sections that follow.

Why marketing should adopt agile

I think we can all agree that companies such as MySpace did not pay enough attention to the changing customer behaviour by listening to what was important to their customers. Then along came Facebook who wiped the floor with them in a matter of years, if not months.

We could also make a similar point about Google cannibalizing the market share of Yahoo and other pre-existing search engines. These stories show us why established companies should be rightly fearful of the next start-up that will take over their customer base without warning - and it will definitely happen if the marketing team is not agile. The only way to prepare your marketing team and your entire organization to deal with the threat of new start-ups is to learn how these start-ups operate and what gives them a competitive advantage over your organization. In all cases it is agile that creates the difference between companies like Spotify and HMV in the entertainment market, or between Airbnb and large hotel chains in the hotel and hospitality market, or Google and Yahoo in the online information and communication market, to mention just a few examples.

If you are still not convinced about why you need your marketing team and your organization as a whole to become agile, I will explain in detail the benefits of becoming an agile marketing organization later on in this chapter. But before we get into that, it would be useful for you to stop and ask yourself: why does my business need to change our current way of working if it is not broken? What is the guarantee that agile marketing will increase business revenue?

We are all aware that the primary aim of marketing is to create successful campaigns in order to either maintain or increase the overall market share of the organization. The marketing process starts with creating customer awareness and then actively engaging customers to ignite and develop their interest in making a purchase of a specific product or service (yours, of course). This process was fairly easy and straightforward before the introduction of technology and the Internet into the marketing process, which has empowered and influenced customers' purchase-decision process and created the 'age of the consumer' as highlighted earlier in this chapter. Advancement in marketing technology, with search engines such as Google, and social-media platforms such as LinkedIn, Facebook and Twitter offering instant information, has improved customer-to-customer communication and interaction. Customers are able to express their opinions and frustrations about brands over the Internet if their pre-purchase expectations were not met after using the product. This, in turn, enables other customers to research and gather product information relatively quickly and directly from those who have previous experience of the same product. As a result, customers are now able to evaluate and review products and services, as well as verify their quality of products through a range of channels, including review websites and price-comparison sites, social media posts and others before making purchase decisions.

Depending on the size of the company and its marketing team, the role of marketing typically involves identifying the target market and creating appropriate customer brand-experience strategies to build demand for products and services. Another side of the marketing coin is also creating and maintaining company reputation by continuously researching customer behaviour and the overall competitor landscape to determine potential strengths and weaknesses to be worked upon. Although it would be easy to dismiss agile marketing as another variety of marketing mumbo jumbo (or some other, equally melodious buzzword), a closer look at start-ups such as Facebook, Netflix and Spotify, which I purposefully mentioned earlier on in the chapter, reveals that these organizations are 100% agile across all of their departments. Google is one of the top companies in terms of marketing, employee engagement and customer loyalty, and its internal culture and organizational structure are completely agile to their very core. Another leader in marketing and overall organizational agility is Airbnb, whose stealth takeover of a good chunk of the hotel market we will be discussing later on in the chapter. If this impressive list of companies is not a good enough reason to at least consider adopting agile across your marketing and other business functions, then let's have a look at how agile can help resolve some of the most common current problems and challenges facing marketing teams, as well as reduce resource wastage, improve the speed of campaign execution and create responsive planning.

Challenges facing marketing teams

Outdated leadership style

The current management style of 'command and control' leadership within marketing teams is counterproductive and does not support the type of innovations being introduced in agile companies such as Google, Spotify and ING bank, to mention just a few. We all recognize that communication between people has evolved from postal letters to emails, and from land lines to mobiles, while the same vertical leadership style that was successful in a former manufacturing era is still being applied to manage marketing teams today. This is particularly inadequate in managing the increasing number of 'millennials' entering today's workforce, as research indicates that 'millennials' prefer a different leadership style to keep them engaged and motivated. Creating an environment that empowers people and gives them a platform to develop their skills has a direct impact on the company's bottom line. How do companies adapt their leadership style and corporate structure to build trust in order to increase employee engagement? Vertical leadership structure is slowly being phased out and replaced with a start-ups' horizontal and inclusive leadership style and we discuss how leaders can adopt an agile approach later on in the chapter.

High-cost and high-risk marketing

Being able to determine the performance of each marketing channel or strategy will help manage the costs associated with marketing campaigns; the inability to do this is causing huge wastage across marketing teams. Some marketing teams do not review or re-evaluate a campaign cost until the end of the financial year, which means that any campaign that is not generating ROI will continue to get funding until the year end. Another important cost centre for marketing teams are external agencies which charge sometimes ridiculously high fees because they are perceived to be the experts, but don't deliver enough of an ROI. We could argue that hiring agencies is directly related to the lack of skill and internal capabilities within marketing teams, due either to the structure of theses teams or the lack of effective and appropriate training methods that would enable existing staff to acquire the required skill set. Let's be clear, I am not saying it is wrong to hire or work with external agencies, I am merely stating that a marketing team can significantly reduce their costs by being agile with their training and development, and by working with agencies in an agile way.

The desire to be able to report on the ROI of a marketing campaign has been a major issue for marketing teams for years, with models such as first click, last click, and other various types being used. For this book, I interviewed one of the web analytics thought-leaders, Jim Sterne, founder of eMetrics Summit and Digital Analytics Association, to get his opinion about attribution modelling, which Jim has been very critical of. According to him, attribution modelling is pretty much useless, due to the fact that the models being proposed are completely artificial. We still cannot determine the effectiveness of each channel and strategy and even machine learning does not guarantee 100% accuracy. Agile marketing is by far the best way to address the issues not resolved through attribution modelling.

Ineffective customer feedback loop

The demise of companies such as Blockbuster begs the question as to whether web analytics data would have flagged up that customers were embracing Spotify and other online streaming services and whether or not this would have enabled them to adapt to the changing customer preferences. However, web analytics data does not provide the reasons behind specific customer behaviour and cannot measure customer experience. Although marketing teams have access to piles and piles of web analytics data and other types of quantitative information about their customers, there is almost no emphasis on the qualitative information. Some marketing professionals rely on the net promoter score, which, in my opinion, is another vanity metric. The most successful and agile companies, such as Google, Spotify and Amazon, follow a 'people first and data second' approach and continuously listen to the qualitative side of customer feedback and this - as we have already seen - makes all the difference in their business success.

Rigid departmental silos

We can all agree that marketing cannot control all aspects of the customer journey across the organization and that it has little or no influence over customer interaction beyond the purchase-confirmation stage, when the customer service department takes over. Another potential problem for marketing teams can be their lack of understanding about the expectations of other departments, such as sales, because of organizational silos caused by internal bureaucracy. Silos can also sometimes exist within marketing teams - this is particularly true in some organizations where teams such as SEO and PPC compete against each other for budgets, amongst other things. In other organizations silos develop due to the difficulty of aligning offline marketing with its online counterpart. If you asked someone in sales or customer service team about their understanding of marketing and the responsibility of the marketing team within the organization, I believe you would hear many different views. The point I am trying to make is that marketing is *not* the responsibility of the marketing team alone, rather it is the whole organization that is responsible for marketing, while the marketing team is simply the 'main owner' of marketing within the organization.

Technological issues

The stack of technological tools available to marketing teams can easily become a problem because marketing teams are usually not as tech-savvy like their IT colleagues. This can sometimes create situations where there are IT teams managing a marketing technology tool without the in-depth understanding of marketing. On the other hand, there also exist marketing professionals without proper understanding of the numerous technological tools available to them. Non-alignment of marketing with IT is another key stumbling block which can be eliminated with agile adoption. Although technology has improved and enhanced the projection of marketing to customers, it has also reduced the human connection between marketing teams and customers. In a bid to get companies better connected with customers, Steve Blanks, the creator of the Customer Development methodology which paved the way for the Lean Startup movement famously said that companies should 'Get out of the building!'. Airbnb started and grew because they connected their customers with accommodation providers on a very personal level, while technology was used only as a means to identify with the customers. When was the last time you and your marketing team had a face-to-face conversation with your customers? The potential of technology to enhance marketing performance is significantly underused, as a lot of marketing professionals believe that web analytics provides all the customer information their marketing teams need. Whilst you can get an abundance of data via web analytics, the fact remains that this quantitative data only tells you what your customers do, it does not explain the why, and the *why*... the *why* is the key to successfully enhancing the customer experience.

Lack of training

In stark contrast with the existing approaches to training and developing marketing team members, Laszlo Bock, in his book *Work Rules*, suggested a completely different approach to employee training, which is based on peer-to-peer training. This is another way that agile can help marketing teams develop their internal skills and leverage outside the training regime in an experiential way. We talked earlier about technology and the need for marketing teams to work with IT to execute marketing campaigns through technology. Skills like SEO and web analytics that used to be IT skills have been embraced by marketing teams, and more marketing professionals need to learn technical skills to be able to harness the full potential that these tools offer them. We will examine the range of technical and non-marketing skills that marketing teams should acquire in order to become fully functional agile marketing teams.

Inflexible budgets

It is absolutely OK to set a budget at the start of the year and assign segments of the budget to each channel or marketing strategy in order to evaluate performance at the end of the year. This approach started before the introduction of the Internet and worked in the era when communication between companies and customers was one directional, from company to customer. With today's rapid changes in customer perception and behaviour, particularly due to information they freely obtain from social media and the Internet, the only way for marketing teams to become truly agile is to introduce flexibility into the marketing budget as a whole.

Rigid planning

Most marketing plans are still being created without any room for change until the end of the fiscal year and, surprisingly, some marketers still confuse marketing strategy with planning. What is your marketing plan? Ask 10 marketing professionals for their definition of a plan and you will possibly get 15 different answers, because we sometimes associate marketing planning with strategies such as SEO, PPC and social media. Later on in this chapter, I offer some examples of how companies like Avaya and Infer Software created and executed agile marketing plans that allowed for flexibility and re-prioritization all through the year - a novel approach. A rigid marketing planning and execution process causes delays to marketing teams and reduces the opportunity to respond to change because everything has to be approved by layers and layers of management - this is about as far from agile as you can get.

How to apply agile to marketing

Before we delve into the application of agile in marketing, I want to share with you a story about Simon Woods, the CMO of Clearvision. This story provides a great example of how a team that had no specific plans to implement agile marketing evolved into agile through their association with the IT department within the organisation. Simon started his role at Clearvision with a small marketing team and quickly realised he inherited a team of people who had no structure to the way they plan, prioritise and execute marketing campaigns. Simon also realised that teams across the organisation: from sales, customer services, product and the rest of the business regularly walked over to marketing staff to have the 'can I have a minute' conversations. Of course, these were just minor conversations between the marketing team and the rest of the organisation but each conversation was creating new tasks which could range from landing page creation or creating a one-page pdf that highlights product USPs, right through to massive event campaign creations that took hundreds of people hours.

Simon realised that there was complete chaos when tasks came into the marketing team from other departments within the business, no structure to how tasks were prioritised or ordered and absolutely no visibility to the rest of the organisation about the extreme workload the marketing team was trying to complete. This lead to frictions and frustrations between the marketing team and the rest of the organisation. While Simon tried explaining to the sales, IT and other managers from external departments that his marketing team is over-worked and over-burdened with every little request coming into the marketing department across the business, these managers were only concerned with making the marketing team complete their marketing related request. Due to having no priority and visibility, Simon's team were struggling to know what to work on first. They were also getting pulled off from what they were working on because new 'important' tasks were being pushed to the marketing team, which resulted in a lot of half-finished tasks.

After assessing the situation of his marketing team and speaking to an agile coach, Simon realised his team's problem was based on lack of time management, responsibility, task completion, sizing and scoping of marketing campaigns, lack of clear project management and the resulting lack of visibility to the rest of the organisation. The agile coach explained to Simon that his team was facing the exact same problem software development teams usually face if they do not adopt agile. So Simon' team started their agile journey with a three-part Kanban board which included the 'To-do', 'Doing' and 'Done' columns. This instantly made everything visible to everyone and external teams began to see the workload of the marketing team which lead to the CEO and another senior manager realising that the team needed to grow, because the current team members didn't have the capacity to execute the existing workload coming in. This resulted in the marketing team growing by 300% in order to cope with the workload.

I asked Simon how he integrated new team members into his agile marketing team. In his opinion, every person coming into the agile marketing team has to make their work visible to everyone else and everyone has to operate through the Kanban board. Simon recommends starting with a 2 week induction process whereby they are trained in how to use Kanban boards and get familiar with the agile rituals. Simon believes agile marketing is very much about the team, strategy and process evolution. Simon created a 30, 60 and 90 days agile marketing training journey for new team members and this also applies to existing team members as well. It essentially the first 30 days is about new members learning about the team process and tools. They learn about which tools the agile marketing team is using, as well as how these tools are being used, whether it's an online Kanban board or cloud tools for storing all the marketing documents. The training journey also involves experiencing the daily meetings, planning meetings and one-to-one review meetings. Simon then introduces the new recruit to other heads of departments like sales, customer service, IT team and the rest of the organisation. Meeting everyone in the business helps new recruits understand how other departments within the business work and how they align with the marketing team, as well as the overall objective of the organisation.

The next 60 days of the induction process is dedicated to teaching the new employee about product features as well as mapping out their personal development plan towards acquiring new skill sets to make them T-shaped marketing professionals. For the first 60 days, Simon assigns the new employee an existing member of the team as a buddy, who is their go-to person in case they have any questions of issues they might need help with. The person assigned to the new employee also shows them around facilities external to the business, such as coffee shops, markets or restaurants that exist in the vicinity of the office. Simon also works personally with the new employees to help them develop into T-shaped marketing professionals and also helps them to create a tailored personal development plan which is agreed with their direct line manager. Every month each individual within the agile marketing team works towards adding a new short-term skill, which is based on their personal preference and professional priorities. For example, some staff could request to be trained in Facebook advertising, content marketing or even learning how to implement an analytics tracking code. This skill training could also be turned into a medium or long-term commitment, such as learning to speak new language or coding skills.

Starting Your Marketing Agility Journey

Henrik Kniberg is the Agile/Lean coach at Spotify and Lego, and his explanation of agile adoption within Spotify aligns well with my own experience and insights from gathered from talking to other agile marketing professionals from around the world.

Agile over Scrum

Scrum is the most popular and most widely used software development framework. However, some agile marketing teams that implemented this framework in their day to day work soon realised that some of the Scrum practices do not neatly fit within the marketing context. Successful agile marketing teams are relaxed about frameworks and are more focused on a change in mindset which will help them understand the core principles of agile and adapt these to their own unique situation.

My own experience and research of agile marketing teams revealed that, although Scrum is still the most popular framework for implementing agile, it is a difficult one for marketing teams to adopt. This is because marketing teams have interdependencies with a range of other departments within an organization and are not as insular as IT software teams. Richard Sheridan, CEO of Menlo Innovations, believes that marketing teams should not force their structure to fit within any particular framework, but they should adapt elements of different frameworks to their team-specific contexts. Creating new roles such as Scrum Master or Product Owner can cause unnecessary stress for teams and this is why most agile marketing teams start with some elements of Kanban mixed with some elements of the Scrum framework. In my opinion, the 'Spotify Model' is tailored to marketing teams, although Henrik Kniberg would also recommend Impact Over velocity. Although agile helps to increase task completion rate, marketers also need to focus on the direct impact of every task on team objectives and, ultimately, on business revenue.

The Lean Startup movement emphasizes prevention of waste in every form: from wasting marketing budgets to wasting time and effort of team members on ineffective marketing strategies. The feedback loop within agile helps teams become streamlined enough to be able to identify waste in time and budget and react quickly to make changes to their marketing plans to correct these errors. This is only possible to achieve if senior management teams empower their marketing teams to make relevant decisions. Daniel Ek, CEO of Spotify, is one of the champions of agile marketing mistakes, as each one of these presents a learning opportunity for the marketing team to get better.

Some marketing teams have become obsessed with vanity metrics, such as conversion rates, website rankings and social media following. Although these are important due to their direct correlation to increasing the revenue of the business, focusing on continuous acquisition of new customers over the improvement of the existing customers' experiences is, ultimately, a flawed approach. Research consistently shows that it costs companies more to attract a new customer than to retain an existing one, and yet in practice a good proportion of marketing teams pay very little attention to customer retention. A successful marketing strategy, therefore, will focus only partly on recruiting new customers, with the bulk of the work focusing on improving customer experience to encourage customers in repeat purchases over a long period of time, which will ensure long-term financial sustainability. The Lean concept is all about providing value to the customer, but it comes with its own Catch 22: whilst it is impossible to measure the customer experience through web analytics data, attempts to understand what customers want through qualitative insights are often ignored due to the lack of 'statistically significant data'.

In the following section I discuss the step-by-step process for adopting agile in marketing which is based on my personal experience of working in agile marketing teams combined with the experience of over 20 agile marketing professionals from all around the world with experience of working in both B2B and B2C marketing teams, whom I interviewed for this book. The discussion covers the process of agile planning, as well as some practical approaches to meetings and the role of rituals in making agile more successful.

Evaluating the company culture

According to Richard Sheridan, CEO of Menlo Innovations, leaders within an organization are the 'stewards of the organizational culture'. They must be clear on who their key stakeholders are and how they need to be served, so that the whole organization implements practices and processes that will aid the achievement of the overall business goals. He is a firm believer that agile marketing teams should focus less on roles and job titles and more on 'servant leadership' that will empower every individual on the team to be proactive in serving the stakeholders and contributing to the achievement of the business objectives.

It is impossible to cover everything there is to know about company culture, but later on in this chapter I will review briefly how companies such as Google and Menloinnovations.com succeeded in creating a healthy company culture. First, we will explore anti-agile company cultures. Before deciding whether or not to adopt agile in your marketing, it is important to conduct an internal assessment of your organization to determine whether your organisation could be classified as a pathological or a bureaucratic one.

A **pathological organization** is one where:

> » individuals within your marketing team or the company hoard information because they don't want any other person to outperform them;

> » teams are motivated by fear and the threat of being fired if they make any mistake or fail to meet their target;

> » senior managers throw junior employees under the bus as scapegoats for everything that goes wrong within the team;

> » this toxic environment causes a great deal of distress to employees due to extreme internal politics.

A **bureaucratic organization** is one where:

> » managers and other senior leaders enjoy micromanaging all teams (including marketing), telling team members how to prioritize and manage their daily tasks;

> » rules and regulations are clearly written, and anything and everything that has not been clearly prescribed must be 'approved' by a committee of managers;

> » rigid processes and company structure do not allow for organizational change, whilst people are oftentimes shuffled around between teams;

> » information and decision-making flows top-down, without transparency and little to no input provided by, or in consultation with, customer-facing employees.

> » encompasses layers and layers of management from top to

bottom, which slows down the information flow and decision-making.

I once worked for a very bureaucratic agency in central London where the seating arrangement was shuffled every two weeks for no specific reason. The senior management team maintained their desk positions, while everybody else was moved around between office floors and sometimes even buildings. Needless to say, this caused a lot of stress to the employees involved and reduced the efficiency of their work performance through no fault of their own. These types of organisations create avoidable problems which drain their resources and increase their costs and will find it very difficult to become truly agile, until they change the overall company culture and approaches to decision-making to demonstrate that they truly value the contribution of every employee.

It is astounding how many companies don't value their employees and their impact on the company's bottom line. Your employees are your best asset and instead of burdening them with layers of bureaucracy, you should be capitalizing on their motivation to work for you and ensuring that it does not diminish due to ineffective company structure and unsupportive corporate culture. In his book, *Drive,* Daniel Pink highlighted three important elements that help harness people's motivation and these are the most important aspects of agile adoption that senior management teams must consider. Although financial incentives (extrinsic motivators) are important for motivating people, they are actually not as effective as harnessing team members' intrinsic motivation by giving them autonomy for their areas of work and involving them in the key decisions made within the team. Drawing on Pink, therefore, we can argue that making marketing teams agile will involve giving their members autonomy over aspects of their work such as:

» what they do;

» when they do it; and

» how they do it.

Agile marketing initiatives will definitely fail without buy-in from C-level executives and this will require a shift from the old-fashioned command-and-control mentality to a new management approach that gives everyone in the marketing team a feeling of autonomy, purpose and the opportunity to achieve mastery in their roles as marketing professionals. Leadership teams in companies such as Google create an atmosphere of trust between the employees and the company by encouraging them to spend 20% of their work schedule on personal projects they find interesting. Such initiatives actually resulted in innovative products such as Gmail and Google News that helped Google take the market by storm, and this was only achieved because their employees had the autonomy to spend their time and energy on things they were passionate about and come up with creative solutions.

Some C-level agile marketing executives such as Michael McKinnon (Global Marketing Operations at Avaya.com) have some of the most successful agile marketing teams. Michael has over seven years of experience in successful implementation of agile marketing across multiple organizations. In my numerous conversations with him, he repeatedly highlighted the importance of giving permission to employees to use 10% of their time on personal tasks each week to reduce employee stress and pressure. In his opinion, senior management should hire people they trust and then give them the freedom and flexibility that allow them to focus on their work. Another option is to employ self-motivated people in your marketing teams because then you can trust these individuals to complete their tasks and be innovative within the team. This further reduces the time you spend managing people and makes for both happy managers and happy marketing teams.

'Psychological safety is a shared belief held by members of a team that the team is safe from interpersonal risk taking'.

Amy Edmondson, Harvard Business School

People should feel confident that they will not be punished or humiliated for expressing their opinions, ideas and concerns and, particularly, that they won't be thrown under the bus. A psychologically safe environment allows people to feel that they can make mistakes and not get fired. Recent research conducted at Google reveals that psychological safety is one of the most important factors that directly impacts on team performance. Google also published data showing an increase of 19% in sales for teams with psychological safety, whereas sales teams without psychological safety experienced a decrease in sales of 19%. Effective implementation of agile requires a culture that encourages transparency by making everyone's Objectives and Key Results (OKR) visible to everyone else in the company. This helps to create accountability, because people can see the organizational-level objectives and how their individual role fits into the overall strategic purpose of the organization. At Google, every employee has access to the OKR of Larry Page and is also empowered to ask questions about how and why certain decisions are made. Every week, Larry and his co-founder Sergey Brin host a meeting that involves all of Google's employees, with thousands attending in person and via video conferencing, while employees who could not attend watch the re-broadcast online. The purpose of the meeting is to update the whole company about new product development, to welcome new recruits, and to have 30 minutes of fielding questions from anyone within the organization on any subject.

Evaluating the company's leadership style

There are very few companies that are 100% agile from top to bottom but Richard Sheridan's company, Menlo Innovations, is a perfect example of a fully agile company. Richard is also the author of the book, *Joy Inc.*, and in my interview with Richard he shared his experience and insight about the importance of the process by which leadership teams can adopt agile across teams and the organization as a whole.

Leaders should be the first to become agile in mindset, by shifting from a command-and-control approach to a more relaxed and inclusive management style. It's easy for leaders to say to themselves: 'I am fine, it's my employees and others within the team who need to go agile'.

Leaders are the ones who can influence a change in the organization's mindset to focus externally on the customers you serve as a business. The teams within the organization should see themselves as servants to the customers. Richard created a team of 12 customer researchers, all high-tech anthropologist, and tasked them with observing their customers' behaviour, habits, goals and vocabulary, in order to design products that will serve these customers. He is of the belief that if marketing teams make a real effort to understand customers in their own environment and context, this will naturally result in joy, both for the customers and for the organization. In order to achieve this, however, it is the leaders within the organization who should be pioneering the mindset of delighting customers and inspiring the rest of the employees to move in that direction. In other words, the goal of the organization has to be focused externally on the customer and leadership teams must be the ones to create the mindset where marketing is the responsibility of the entire organization because customers don't interact just with the marketing department, but a range of other departments within the organization at different points in time. When a company truly embraces an agile mindset, they start rethinking everything they do, they start doing things differently. The greatest shift in mindset happens when people stop thinking about 'what is the size of my office and my budget?'. Only when people stop focusing only on their own silos, can we begin working and achieving together as human beings and this will only happen when the customer becomes the factor that aligns the whole organization. This is the agile mindset that leaders need to adopt and transmit to the entire organization.

Agile coaching and the pilot team

It is important understand that there will be an element of customization of existing agile principles and practices to marketing. This is why it is important to hire a very good agile coach who understands agile in the context of marketing, or - at least - in a context different to IT. Agile has been so successful in IT because IT teams are particular about hiring agile coaches with the appropriate understanding. Marketing

teams are different from IT teams in terms of interdependencies with other parts of the organization and so, in order to turn your marketing agile, you will need to hire a professional agile coach with an in-depth understanding of marketing, as well as some experience of facilitating and coaching marketing teams. Although there are books, videos and online training materials about frameworks such as Scrum, Kanban and others, these resources alone will not be enough. One of the reasons I wrote this book was for it to serve as the agile marketing support resource for teams and individuals to understand the process of becoming agile. There are relevant real-life case studies of agile marketing implementation in a range of contexts presented in the final section of this book, which should give you some insight into some of the challenges, benefits and approaches to implementing agile in different marketing contexts. In the absence of financial viability to hire a coach, I am hoping that this book will help you along the way to introducing agility to your marketing function.

When looking for an agile coach, an organization should consider the term agility as an organizational term that means engendering and growing hearts, minds and physical practices towards being agile and implementing agile ways of working in the organization. This person must also be an effective influencer and have a high level of emotional intelligence to be sensitive to individuals' circumstances and changes that may be occurring in different areas of the organization. With this in mind, when recruiting an Agile Coach, Sam Zawadi advisesyou should search for two main kinds of expertise:

» Expertise in agility

» Expertise in coaching

Expertise in agility

An agile coach should have a deep knowledge, understanding and practice of at least one Agile method or framework. The ability to sense the agile maturity levels in teams and the organization is critical to calibrating agility to fit the context of that specific organization,

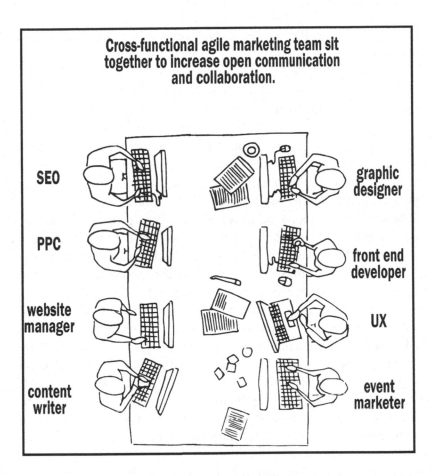

Cross-functional agile marketing team sit together to increase open communication and collaboration.

and using that as the reference point to let the organization grow and adapt. The Agile Coach should be able to describe, in simple language, the benefits of having agility within the organization: the 'why' we are doing this, not just the 'way' we are doing this. The Agile community is a lively and active one, with many meet ups and events occurring globally. Agile Coaches who are passionate about their art will attend these events regularly, read the latest books and articles, and sometimes be an active writer or speaker themselves, which can provide an insight into the kind of personalities they have and their views and opinions on certain subjects. Many well rounded Agile Coaches also carry additional qualifications from different Agile frameworks and methods, and therefore have the ability to tailor and shape agility to the context of their respective organizational requirements.

Expertise in coaching

An agile coach should bean emotionally intelligent person who is able to create intelligent teams that think and adapt quickly to the context in which they are functioning. Look for individuals who are expert listeners, respectful, non-judgmental and unconsciously competent. He or she should espouse what is known as active servant-leadershipand be able to recognize the team as a system that operates within the greater whole, as well as be aware of the direction that this whole is taking. The coach must be able to allow the team to find their own voice, listen to what that voice is saying and respond accordingly. This helps nurture and further grow the teams' intelligence and their way of being together so that they may flourish while working together.The agile coach is always a pragmatist, a practical person who can hold up the metaphorical mirror to the team, and allow them to see and sense themselves, the way they are, and what is happening in the team at that moment, helping and inspiring them along the way. Finally, look for a coach who continuously assesses and adapts themselves, in order not to represent an impediment to the team's progress. Coaching qualifications are useful to ascertain that the person is not only proficient in practicing agility, but also in coaching human beings and systems of human beings (teams and organizations), however, this it is by no means a prerequisite.

When a coach helps create a team, or when they join a new team, it is a good idea to examine how the team wants to be together as they do their work; the being and the doing should correlate to the agile values and principles. However, deeper than that, the being and the doing should also describe how team members want to talk and act with one another. Sometimes this may conflict with agile values and principles, other times it will be a perfect match, other times still it may be somewhere in between. Some questions agile coaches should be asking the team include: 'what kind of atmosphere and environment do you want to have?', 'how do you prefer to challenge and support each other?', 'what will make you excel and flourish as a team'?, 'is there anything you will reject as a team? 'What are the kinds of things you are prepared to accept as a team?', and so on. In order to be able to answer these questions honestly, the team will require a sense of psychological safety and trust and will need to feel empowered. For example, an individual in a team might feel safe enough to think that, 'it's okay to say what I want to say right now, because I know I will not be judged, even if I am wrong'. The coach should be able to provide this sense of safety and security by facilitating the creation of a team agreement that describes the way the team wants to be together and the qualities, values and principles they want to share with each other and abide by. This could be a simple bullet pointed list that forms a Team Contract that is regularly revisited, discussed and adapted as new people enter or leave the team, or as the atmosphere and the environment around the team changes. It is therefore necessary to update the Team Contract as the team grows and changes over time.

After hiring a coach, the next step is to create a pilot team made up of volunteers from your existing marketing team. It is important to give people the freedom to join the team and not force them into taking part. These individuals will then be trained by the coach to make sure they understand the agile values and principles before being introduced to a range agile frameworks. The pilot team should be allowed to decide which agile framework or mix of frameworks they will be comfortable working with. The leadership team is also part of this initial training, which normally lasts between two and three full days. The agile coach will train everyone on the team and leaders will learn everything they need to know about the Scrum, Kanban and Spotify models. It also important to make sure you retain the same agile coach who trained the team to guide your entire agile marketing transformation.

Michael McKinnon, whom we mentioned earlier in this chapter, started his agile marketing process by allowing everyone on the team to become familiar with the agile rituals, values and principles. The first three months of the process were dedicated to ongoing training and actually working with everyone on the team to slowly change their mindset towards becoming agile without adding any stress or pressure to his team. In a time of big organizational changes, it is important to have that one constant to help you successfully navigate the challenging times.

Defining top-down objectives and key results

While the marketing plan for the year is normally created at the start of the fiscal year, the agile marketing team also schedules quarterly planning meetings to review the activities of the current quarter and make any necessary changes to the marketing plan for the next quarter. During the quarterly meeting every member of the online and offline marketing teams maps out their own activities and tasks for the next quarter with an emphasis on how all the team members' activities align with each other. I was recently involved in an agile marketing team's quarterly planning and we had everyone on the team prepare their plans and projections for the quarter. Members of the Search Marketing, Social Media, Conversion Optimisation, Email Marketing and Analytics, Customer Experience and Website Admin teams gathered together for a 2-day face to face meeting to discuss the breakdown of the work for the quarter. Everyone presented their plan with detailed conversations about dependencies between each individual's activities and the overall marketing team's work. The aim of the meeting was to identify the issues with the IT department that were causing delays, as well as to understand exactly how the activities of external agencies, working on the SEO and PPC campaigns for the organisation, were overlapping with our own internal team activities. This is an example of the new Objectives - Key Results framework (also known as OKR). OKR is a framework that allows individuals within the agile marketing team to align and connect their objectives and tasks with their core team, the wider department and rest of the organization, thus allowing employees to improve their performance. Although OKR first started at Intel, a large number of reputable brands are currently adopting the framework as well: companies such as Oracle, Twitter, LinkedIn, Spotify, Eventbrite and Zynga. John Doerr first introduced the OKR framework to Google when it was a company

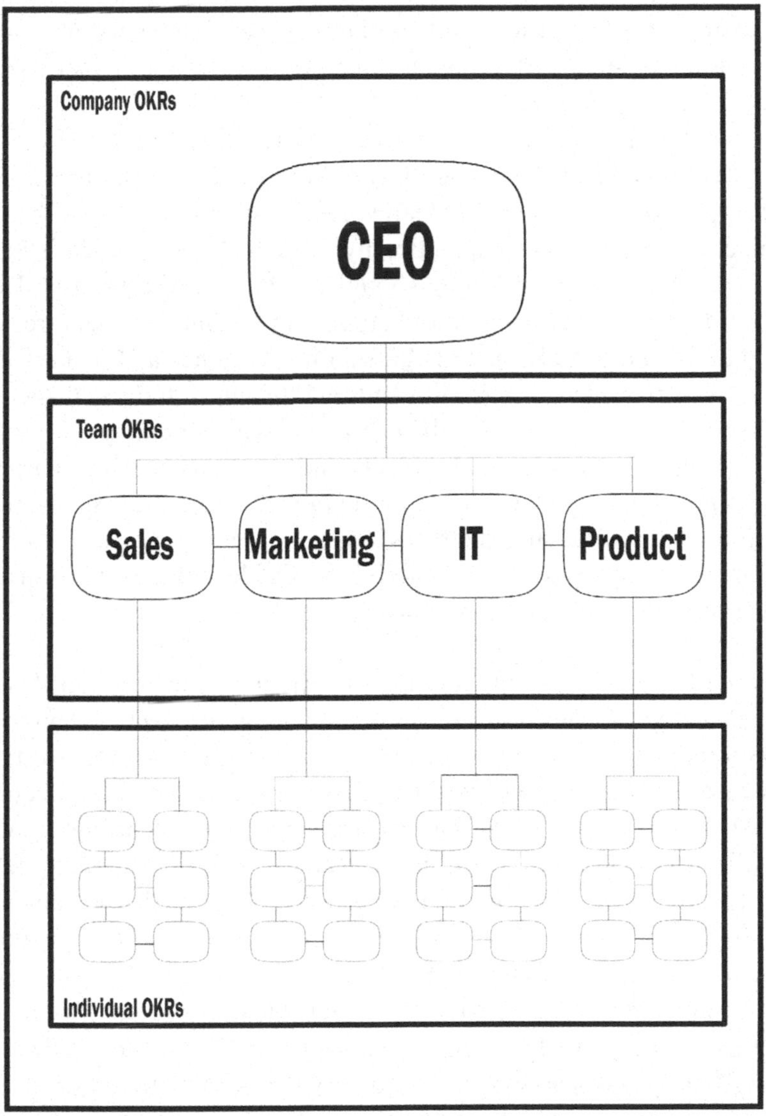
Company OKRs
CEO
Team OKRs
Sales
Marketing
IT
Product
Individual OKRs

with just around 40 employees and this model is still being used at Google today. It is a framework that allows for better flexibility in responding to the changes in the external environment and consumer preferences, in order to minimize the wastage of financial and other resources on strategies and tactics that do not create sufficient ROI.

So what is an objective? Objectives define, in a very specific way, what an individual or the team wants to achieve in each quarter. For example, the objective for search-engine marketing could be 'to increase new customer acquisition by 10% in Q1'. Objectives should have a clear end point – they should not be an ongoing task. They should also be inspiring, motivating and qualitative. Key results should be measurable, metrics based on milestones and quantitative data. For example, a key result would be 'to launch three new themes for the website blog that will impact on search rankings, improve page-load time and internal website links'. OKRs are set quarterly and annually across the marketing team and across the organization. Agile teams make sure their OKR are measurable, set at personal, team and company level, and publicly available to the entire team and everyone else within the company.

We will now look at how a C-Level agile marketing thought-leader implemented OKR from an agile marketing perspective and how OKR aligns with other departments and the whole organization. Sean Zinsmeister is Vice President Product Marketing at Infer.com, a predictive sales and marketing software company. According to him, it all starts with goals. Each fiscal year the executive team presents wide-ranging goals to the company. Flexible, annual priorities and quarterly objectives allow marketing teams to be more agile, stretch themselves and stay focused on executing campaign tasks. This company-wide OKR document is uploaded to Google Docs for easy sharing across the entire organization with the aim of creating a culture of transparency, so that everyone in the company can see the departmental, team and individual OKRs of everyone else in the organization. The document contains and restates the organization's mission and vision, which are easy to understand, and instructs new employees or contractors about the products and services being created and the go-to marketing strategy. Fiscal annual goals are broken down into company-wide OKR, to which all the department-level OKRs will roll up. The agile marketing team at Infer.com operated on the fiscal year versus the calendar year; this is a decision many companies such as Salesforce and Google have also chosen for their operating plans. Company-wide OKR, by definition, touch all of the departments in the organization. For example, in FY17, the company-wide OKR is to make the new release of profile management platform for general availability. There are sub-tasks beneath, which are the key to the success of this OKR.

OKR example; general release of the profile management platform:

A. Get x number of customer stories.

B. Get team fully trained and certified.

C. X number of deployments live.

The other OKRs take on a similar style, but note the numbering after each sub-objective. At the end of each quarter, each will be scored as to how well it performed, which is one of the ways Infer.com measures success, in addition to its revenue goals and other key business metrics. Since each company-wide OKR is cross-departmental, each department submits their OKRs before the start of each quarter, while the department heads then agree upon the department-level OKRs with the executive team. This methodology allows for everything to be rolled up at the end of each quarter as listed below:

FY Goals

Quarterly Company OKRs

Quarterly Department OKRs

Before the end of every quarter, departments give feedback regarding the score of their OKRs depending on the confidence of their performance. Google Docs is a very effective tool for the marketing team at Infer.com because it allows everyone on the team to link company OKRs to the department level and then to individual team member's OKR, so that they can be navigated and explored by anyone in the company. This type of transparency is key for the agile marketing team. In this way, one person within the marketing team always has a reference for what the others are doing, which promotes accountability across the team, regardless of job function, and creates a shared sense of contribution to the organization.

OKRs provide a framework for marketing to execute, because you are setting an objective and going after it as a team. Agile marketing teams need to have something to aim for as they execute campaigns without disconnecting from the overall objectives of the organization. According to Sean Zinsmeister, structuring tasks into sprints works well for agile marketing teams because it builds a natural cadence into the working week, where everyone on the team begins each week with a set objective and they don't have to deviate from it, which makes them more focused in their work. With OKR, it is necessary to have a combination of top-down and bottom-up planning. Planning to determine an appropriate budget allocation to each marketing channel in the customer purchase-decision path, to schedule task duration to execute the marketing plan and the achieve the expected ROI requires the combined input of top leadership in collaboration with the bottom-level team members, who are able to offer rich insights from their client-facing activities. At Avaya.com, Michael McKinnon has his marketing teams spread across multiple continents in different time zones, so he creates a team-level OKR and then empowers the rest of his agile marketing team to create their personal OKRs to align with the overall OKR of the marketing team.

A good agile marketing plan is updated throughout the year so that it always reflects current expectations from customer segments. As part of the collaborative planning approach, agile marketing teams use daily stand-up meetings to discuss and coordinate task execution during the day. Planning during daily meetings allows team members to reassess and reevaluate the OKRs in their schedule to synchronize them to the overall team objectives. OKR best practice for agile marketing professionals requires that everyone on the agile marketing team creates their OKRs in the first week of each quarter. They are also expected to align their individual-level OKRs with the team's OKR and review these during one-on-one meetings with the CMO (Chief Marketing Officer) or during team meetings. Listed below are the steps you and your team can take to implement OKRs:

>> Identify the marketing team's objectives and key results. For large organizations, the CMO should collaborate with team leaders to draft team-level objectives.

>> Roll out OKRs to the entire marketing team and organization.

>> Work with individuals within the marketing team to define their individual OKRs which will contribute to the overall marketing-team OKRs.

>> Agree and finalize the final OKR plan with everyone on the team.

If you are interested in learning more about OKRs for your agile marketing team, I recommend the book *Objectives and Key Results* by Paul R. Niven and Ben Lamorte.

Creating a team working agreement

Defining acceptable behaviour between individuals within the agile marketing team is extremely important. Every team member needs to understand the rules of engagement, such as 'no name calling' or 'no inappropriate jokes'. From a team perspective, adopting agile marketing starts with the creation of a team working agreement, which helps team members to develop a shared culture built around the overall objective of the team and learn how to align their individual objectives with those of the team. All members of the agile marketing team then write down important rules and regulations that each person feels is important for them to work successfully as a collaborative and cross-functional team. These team norms and rules exist to provide reference material for when conflicts arise within the team.

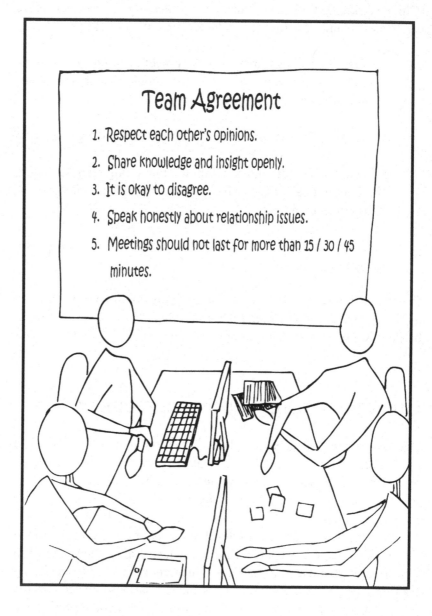

The only way to resolve conflicts between individuals in agile marketing teams is to encourage team members to have an open conversation about conflicts. This helps to build a culture of open communication, honesty, trust, and respect across the whole team. Working agreements help members to be more self-aware about their behaviour and understand when it conflicts with the working agreement accepted by everyone on the team. For example, if the working agreement indicates that people should not interrupt each other when communicating, this helps to draw attention to such behaviour if it occurs during team meetings. Working agreements are also important to establish a set of behavioural standards as to how team members will work together. This common set of rules that all team members abide by helps team members to develop a sense of shared responsibility, increase members' awareness of their own behaviour, and empower the facilitator to lead the group according to their mutual agreement. These agreements should be created to fit the context of a specific agile marketing team. Below is an example of points from a team agreement of an agile marketing team Sam Zawadi worked with recently:

» As a team we trust each other's expertise and suggestions

» We support each other wherever we can to ensure the health and safety of the team

» As individuals in the team, we can ask questions about things we don't understand without being or feeling judged

» As a team, we can rely on each other for support through challenging times

» As a team, we like to bring some fun to our everyday working practices

» We think as a team, and we are sensitive to what we as a team are saying

» As a team, we practice agile ways of working and we think

as an agile team

» Where we do not have all the answers, we will seek them out

We support each other's pursuit of knowledge and relentlessly strive to continuously improve.

Organizing a Kanban board (to-do list)

After interviewing more than 50 agile coaches working in both marketing and IT, combined with my personal experience of working in agile marketing teams, I can state with certainty that the process of adopting agile in marketing is totally different from that for IT software teams because of the differences in processes, people, skill requirements, personalities and technology. It is important to respect the existing processes, roles and responsibilities when introducing agile to a marketing team. This will reduce the stress and anxiety associated with change initiatives. Agile adoption must start from an individual team member's level before growing organically to the team level, rather than being restricted to an entire team-adoption approach.

Some teams start their agile marketing journey by adopting Scrum, which is not necessarily the best approach for marketing teams. In my personal opinion, Kanban is by far the easiest way to implement agile marketing, whether you're talking about small or large, as well as collocated or multinational teams - it works in so many different contexts. 'Kanban' is a Japanese word which means 'billboard' or 'signal board' and it was originally used for inventory control within Toyota manufacturing plants to improve manufacturing efficiency. Kanban boards today have a wide application in a range of industries outside motor manufacturing. They are particularly useful in allowing the marketing team to visualize the flow of their tasks, which then highlights any slow-moving task which result from obstacles. They also help team members to better understand their own work capacity because they are able to work on one task at a time, which eliminates switching between tasks and improves their focus and efficiency.

Creating a Kanban board from the perspective of an individual and a team is fairly straightforward. All you need is a whiteboard within the office that is divided into columns such as 'To-Do', 'Doing' and 'Done', as well as post-it cards/sticky notes to document the individual tasks that will be posted on the board. The columns of your Kanban board should be based on the context of your team and should not be limited to the column titles stated above, although I would recommend using the 'To-Do', 'Doing' and 'Done' columns to start with, until you are comfortable adapting the board to the context of your team. For geographically distributed marketing teams, you have the option of using online Kanban boards such as kanbanize.com, trello.com and leankit.com.

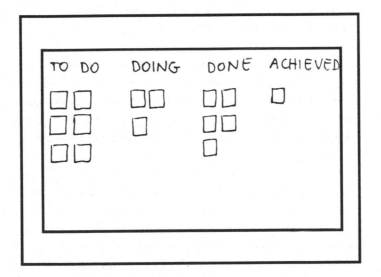

An example of a Kanban board

The Kanban board creates transparency and visibility that are necessary for improved communication between individuals within the marketing team, while also allowing a visual understanding about dependencies with other parts of the organization. This helps to reduce the wastage associated with task duplication between team members. For example, although keyword research in SEO is not exactly the same as in paid search advertising, there is some duplication in this task, and a visual representation of what everyone is doing can lead to open discussions about how team members can collaborate on similar tasks to reduce any waste of time and waste of marketing dollars. Creating a Kanban board is easy if you follow these steps:

» Create a list (backlog) of *all* the tasks that you normally work on; this should include tasks you are currently working on and tasks that you work on occasionally. The aim of this activity is to start to visualize all the tasks your marketing team is currently working on. This activity does not have to be completed at the first attempt; you can update the list with new tasks as you remember them.

» Group similar marketing tasks together into a cluster of related tasks. For example, you can group all SEO-related tasks into one cluster, and other channel-specific tasks into another cluster. This will encourage a culture of continuous improvement and collaboration between team members.

» Identify where work is entering your to-do list in order to make sure that whoever is passing on this task to you understands that you have a limit to the amount of work you are able to work on at any particular time. Improving the quality of work completed by marketing teams means that everyone on the team needs to set and understand the capacity at which each team member is able to complete a task, as well as how many tasks they are able to work on within a week. When new tasks are added into the to-do list, these tasks will automatically join a queue, which means that only important tasks with direct impact on ROI will be moved to the 'Doing' column.

» Update the 'To-Do' column with tasks that you plan to work on each week, while making sure that you do not overburden yourself with tasks you are not able to complete within the week in a bid to impress your boss. Adding too many tasks into your Kanban board will only create stress and anxiety for you.

» On day one, start working on one task, which means that you take a single task from the 'To-Do' column into the 'Doing' or 'In-Progress' column and you make sure that you don't start working on another task until you have fully completed the one in the 'Doing' column; this is known as 'limiting work in progress'. This approach focuses on eliminating multitasking, which is counter-productive because of the stress associated with switching from one task to another and the waste of time involved when trying to constantly refocus your attention between the two.

» As tasks flow through the board from 'To-Do', to 'Doing', to 'Done' (completed), the next question is: who do I deliver the completed task to? Before you start working on any task, it is important to have a clear picture about the benefits, and whom or where the completed task will be delivered to. This is called 'identifying handoffs' of tasks between team members and external teams and these enable the team to get a better understanding of where a completed task from one team member is transferred to someone else within the team or to external agencies. For example, the content team submits content to the website team responsible for creating landing pages, or a web analytics member of the team working on tracking codes will eventually deliver the code to the IT or website team for implementation.

» As tasks flow through the board from 'To-Do', to 'Doing', to 'Done', there might be delays to some tasks due to dependencies on other team members or external resources. It is important to highlight the friction points affecting task-completion flow, and it is the responsibility of the leader of the team to remove these friction points.

» Finally, as a team, it is also important to keep a close eye on the total work in progress (WIP) to make sure that all team members are aware of the total of completed tasks. From speaking to Richard Sheridan, CEO of Menlo Innovations, I know that he recommends that agile marketing teams start with a physical Kanban board because he believes that his teams work better and more collaboratively when tasks are displayed on physical boards, rather than digital ones, however, this is not going to be possible for geographically scattered teams. At the end of the day, you have to find a way that works for you and your team.

Starting agile team rituals

In this section we focus on understanding what a sprint means as an activity and recognize the importance of creating sprint goals and a prioritized sprint task list.

What is a sprint?

Campaign implementation tasks in the marketing plan are organized in iterations, or cycles of one to four calendar weeks; these are called *sprints*. The sprint is always meant to have a time-boxed and consistently short duration to encourage continuous learning and adaptation of the marketing plan. A good sprint also starts with a defined target, which is referred to as 'Definition of Done'. This encompasses the acceptance criteria specified by the marketing leadership (CMO/product owner), i.e. it spells out when a task can be considered completed, in order to be able to move on to the next one.

Sprint principles

In order to foster the team culture of openness and transparency, teams are encouraged to follow the following sprint principles:

» The entire team is responsible for sprint planning through collaborative thinking and estimation.

» The duration of the sprint should be long enough to complete the tasks set at the beginning of the sprint.

» Sprints also need to be short enough to be reviewed and adapted.

» Sprints should be locked-in, with minimal interruptions during their executions, which will maximize the levels of concentration of team members.

» The whole team is accountable for the outcome of the sprint. This will help to reduce the finger-pointing and support a culture of open collaboration.

» The team should hold daily stand-up meetings for the duration of the sprint in order to identify any issues or hindrances that might affect work progress during the sprint.

Sprint tasks (user stories)

Everyone in the team creates a multiple task card (user stories) to describe tasks to be completed during the sprint. The card is not meant to capture the detailed information about the activity to be performed, but rather to capture the essence of the task to be completed. It reduces any form of misunderstanding because the content of the task card is visible to everyone, which allows further clarification questions from people within the team who do not understand the purpose of the task.

A common template for a task card is in the form of a sticky note attached to the Kanban board, (task board) which explains the activity with reference to the expected outcome of the task, for example, 'Complete the broad match keyword research for the website homepage. The keyword list developed will be added to the Valentine's Day PPC campaign'.

Sprint goals

Sprint goals in agile marketing define what success looks like at the end of the sprint. These are the acceptance criteria agreed between the CMO (Product Owner) and each team member at the beginning of the sprint. We all agree on the contribution of each of the sprint's goals to the overall KPI as stated in the marketing plan in terms of adding value to the company. Activities and tasks within the sprint are then structured to achieve the sprint goal at the end of the sprint. For example, the sprint goal for a new website redesign project might be data gathering to understand website usability issues. At the end of the sprint, the CMO will be presented with detailed documentation of insights gathered during the sprint. The sprint goal is also a checklist of the type of tasks the team is expected to complete at the end of the sprint.

The sprint goal allows for clarification by providing additional details of how the list of tasks within the sprint contributes towards achieving the objectives specified in the marketing plan. It allows the CMO to reaffirm his/her expectations from members of the agile marketing team at the end of the sprint. Because this is a face-to-face conversation or virtual communication between the CMO and each member of the team, there is less miscommunication and fewer misunderstandings that are prevalent in email and other forms of electronic communication. The sprint goal is then, ultimately, an agreement between the CMO and each member of the agile marketing team with regard to the expected deliverables at the end of each sprint. Having a clear goal for a sprint allows every member of the team to focus on all the tasks they need to complete in order for the team to achieve the agreed sprint goals. It also reduces anxiety and misunderstanding across the team because everyone is aware of the goal at the start of the sprint – with less likelihood that the sprint goal will change before the end of the sprint. This is what makes agile unique.

Time-boxing

Agile marketing teams work in a time-management mindset and framework that encourages strict and consistent start-date and end-date rules for marketing campaigns. For example, inside a time-box of 15 minutes for a daily meeting, the team is expected to hold the meeting for exactly 15 minutes so as to maintain a culture of disciplined timekeeping. We are all guilty of attributing financial cost alone while ignoring the fact that time is also a cost element in marketing worth considering. This is why time-boxing is required in agile marketing:

No perfection required

There is no perfect campaign in agile marketing and it is important to reduce the expectations of the team in terms of planning. The expectation of perfection increases the time spent in planning the sprint and creates stressful pressure for members of the team, which ultimately reduces their ability to perform their work in an agile way.

Shows progress

Time-boxing sprints also helps to measure progress towards marketing targets through a review meeting at the end of the sprint to understand and gather feedback about how much value was created.

Limits work-in-progress

Multitasking by trying to complete a large number of tasks simultaneously is one of the problems of traditional marketing. The time-boxing of sprints and tasks allocated to each individual during the sprints helps to limit the number of work-in-progress tasks during a sprint. At the start of a sprint, teams plan and prioritize the number of tasks that each individual will perform in order to reduce surprises, which are the main source of work-related stress for team members.

Increases motivation

Team members are motivated during the sprints because all the tasks allocated for the sprint have been assessed by each member based on their estimation of the time required to finish each task. My experience is that most marketing tasks are easily completed as a result of knowing the end date of the sprint and being assured about the low likelihood of unexpected tasks being thrown at me during the sprint.

Generates feedback

Structuring marketing tasks into sprints generates fast feedback loops to inform changes in the allocation of budgetary funds and task prioritization based on customer insights. During each sprint we create a list of tasks to be completed by everyone on the team and then we have the opportunity to inspect and adapt based on how they meet the KPI targets set at the start of the sprint.

Enables adaptive planning

Structuring marketing tasks into sprints makes it easier to plan and make changes to marketing plans based on customer feedback from web analytics, CX and UX data. It is easier to plan for a single month with a clear understanding of tasks that the team needs to complete, rather than the quarter of the full year. Furthermore, owing to the volatile and ever-changing nature of marketing technology and channels, planning for short sprints requires less effort and entails less risk, because the team has the ability to change and adapt the marketing plan iteratively.

Multiple checkpoints

Structuring marketing tasks and campaigns into sprints provides frequent checkpoints to evaluate cost of acquisition of new customers, as well as to review engagement and retention cost.

Agile team structure

Agile marketing team structure is essential to the success of marketing initiatives, which impact significantly on the business revenue streams. In this section we discuss the structure of agile marketing teams, documentation and tools needed, as well as the structure of the team meetings.

Agile marketing teams are made up of leadership and implementation team levels. Strategic decisions that involve planning and budget allocation to different marketing channels fall under the leadership of the Chief Marketing Officer and other senior stakeholders who are nominated for the Product Owner role. The Head of Digital, or anyone else who is directly responsible for managing junior-level team members, will then be assigned as the Scrum Master. Individuals who are responsible for daily optimization of different marketing channels, such as search engine optimization (SEO), paid search advertising (PPC), social-media marketing and others, form the implementation team. This implementation team is the marketing equivalent of the development team in agile software development.

Agile marketing teams must work with other stakeholders within the business, as well as with external marketing agencies, which makes them different from agile software teams, which are rather insular in nature. Agile marketing teams have two main characteristics:

1.   They are self-organizing

The agile marketing team is collaborative, self-organizing and driven by customer insights based on qualitative (CX/UX) and quantitative (analytics) data. By definition, self-organization is the ability to respond to complex team-level issues by acting and reacting to changes in marketing trends. Control of strategy-level marketing tasks is decentralized from senior management. Team members responsible for different marketing channels choose how best to optimize the performance of their marketing channel with consideration of how these channels affect other marketing channels and the overall marketing strategy.

2.   They are cross-functional

Generalizing-specialist is the best way to describe the nature of agile marketing teams because all skills required for the successful completion of a marketing campaign must always be available within the team. Cross-functional agile marketing teams encourage members to acquire broader skill sets in online and digital marketing. For example, a search advertising expert on the team is encouraged to learn and understand social-media marketing and content marketing, with the overall aim of increasing the skills and competencies across the whole agile marketing team. This model is one of the major reasons why the agile framework has been very successful in the IT industry and why it can work in marketing, too. Increasing the skills required to accomplish marketing strategies without over-reliance on any one single team member can increase the flexibility, teamwork and inter-dependence among team members and have a positive impact on the team's overall performance.

These two characteristics, as described above, are designed to encourage adaptability, flexibility and continuous improvement in the mindset needed in an agile marketing environment.

Skill distribution

Agile teams must be stable and dedicated to their task to maintain focus. Agile marketing teams also try to be collated and empowered to make decisions as long as those decisions are within the boundaries of the marketing plan. Team members must be self-motivated and demonstrate this by not always waiting for their line manager's direction on which task to complete and how. The team is focused on an agreed set of KPIs and how these will be achieved. Open and honest communication is also encouraged across the team, which is often reflected in the open-plan seating arrangement recommended for agile marketing. No finger-pointing is allowed within the team: members are mutually accountable to each other, which helps to reduce the politics within the team. Agile team members work together to reduce waste in terms of both marketing budgets and time. Yes, time is expensive and agile marketing teams focus on reducing activities that consume their time without adding value to the marketing objectives. Every agile marketing team needs people with skills in customer experience and user experience, which help to maximize the value of customer feedback to inform change in marketing strategy when required. This role normally sits within external departments separate from the marketing team but the blurring of the lines between marketing and IT demands that agile marketing teams develop the skills and capability required for UX and CX functions, in order to make the team fully cross-functional and self-organizing.

Chief marketing officer – CMO (Product Owner)

Each marketing team needs a strategy-oriented person at Board level to interpret and deliver the overall company objectives from a marketing perspective. In the agile marketing team, this person is called the Product Owner. Depending on the size and structure of the marketing team, the product owner is normally the most senior person in the marketing function who serves as the intermediary between marketing and the rest of the organization.

The Product Owner does not need to have detailed knowledge of marketing strategy implementation; they are focused only on the strategic aspect of marketing that involves the creation of the overall integrated marketing strategy. For example, the Product Owner (CMO) does not need to create the detailed content of the marketing strategy: they just need to know a little about content calendars, but a lot about the business value of content marketing to the customer's buying decisions.

The CMO is responsible for creating the marketing plan (product backlog), which includes the KPIs for every marketing channel. As mentioned earlier in this chapter, the product backlog is a prioritized list of marketing channels that the marketing team is expected to implement during each quarter of the year. It is the responsibility of the CMO to make sure that each item of the marketing plan is easily understandable to each member of the agile marketing team, including how it impacts their role.

The CMO should communicate effectively with all stakeholders external to the marketing team and use the relevant customer information gathered to keep the marketing plan updated from a customer-insight perspective. The CMO understands the business from a strategic perspective, so they can rank each strategy within the marketing plan based on expected return on investment (ROI) and any other factor that the company shareholders find relevant. Items in the marketing plan are then prioritized based on their value of generating new customers and retaining existing ones. The higher they are on the list, the sooner they will be executed by the implementation team. The entire team must respect the decision of the CMO as being final – no one should be allowed to override the decision of the CMO. In situations where the CMO lacks the knowledge to make informed decisions about marketing strategy, it is normal to delegate such decision-making responsibilities to the most experienced and qualified member of the agile marketing team.

Head of Digital/Offline Marketing (Scrum Master)

Both my research and my experience have revealed that some teams appoint the most senior member of the team as the Scrum Master; this individual is usually someone with hands-on experience and understanding of different marketing channels, who helps members of the marketing team through coaching. Being familiar with both Scrum and Kanban is a must for this particular role because they will be responsible for training and coaching the rest of the marketing team. Aside from coaching the team in their preferred agile framework, this person is also responsible for removing any impediments faced by the implementation team, facilitating sprint-review meetings and providing training to new members of the team to help them understand different agile methodologies and how they apply to marketing. The Scrum Master will also help external stakeholders to understand the appropriate interaction with the agile marketing team while also helping to lead the organization in its efforts to adopt agile across all the other departments (in the case of organization-wide agile adoption).

The marketing team (campaign implementation team)

Agile marketing implementation teams are similar to those the development teams within agile software development. The implementation team is made up of subject-matter experts in customer acquisition, engagement, retention and advocacy. They are responsible for implementing items in the overall marketing plan and managing changes in the team plan according to customer insights gathered through CX, UX and web analytics.

Implementation team members should be cross-functional and skilled in more than one single marketing channel. They should be self-organizing and able to structure their own workload without depending on their line manager for directions. A task or marketing channel might be assigned to a single member throughout the sprint, but other members of the agile marketing team should also posses the skills necessary to complete the same task if required. No individual in an agile marketing team should be indispensable.

The implementation team delivers the KPI target for each marketing channel at the end of each sprint as defined in the marketing plan. It is strongly recommended that each member of the team work full-time on a single channel, so as to stay focused and agile.

Agile marketing planning

Let us look at why traditional (non-agile) marketing plans often fail. A critical problem for a traditional marketing plan is that it focuses on customer insights at the start of a campaign without allowing changes to the scope of the plan to cater for changes in market conditions, until the end of the fiscal year, when a new plan is created for the following year. Plans are documented performance projections of how we believe each marketing channel will perform against set KPI targets. Agile marketing encourages a mindset that puts emphasis on continuous planning as opposed to having a definitive marketing plan at the start of a campaign. The uncertainty surrounding attribution models and the ongoing discovery of new customer touch points validate the need for updating marketing plans based on new insights gained through the course of the execution of the marketing plan.

Understanding the marketing channel, or mix of channels, that converts prospects into customers is one of the major problems facing marketing teams. Although marketing attribution models try to provide much-needed answers to channel and strategy performance, this information is not always readily available when creating marketing plans or campaigns. Hence, we make assumptions during planning based on past experiences, previous data and our own gut feeling. Traditional marketing then adopts the principles of fixed cost, scope and time, which is perfect for campaigns that are predictable, such as event planning and marketing campaigns that target special occasions like Valentine's Day and Christmas. However, for marketing campaigns involving search marketing and other channels that provide less predictability, we need to ensure that although cost and duration of the marketing plan are fixed, the scope needs to be updated continuously in order to maintain flexibility.

Marketing plans help us to know what budget needs to be available for each and every marketing channel during a campaign, quarter, or a full fiscal year. Plans also help us to know whether we are meeting our agreed KPIs and the contribution of each channel to the overall strategic objectives. However, changing customer perceptions, technology and competitive landscape make marketing planning more and more difficult, which is why initial plans agreed at the start of the financial year are often no longer relevant by the time our plan comes to its end. We often ask ourselves as marketing professionals how can we get an accurate estimation of budget entries for each marketing channel with the associated ROI metrics to validate our marketing plan, i.e. how do we attribute ROI to specific marketing channels?

Agile marketing is not just about determining an appropriate plan for each marketing channel or strategy mix. It aims to understand customer requirements by identifying the right insights as input and then integrating this input into the agile marketing process adapted to frameworks like Scrum, Kanban or the Waterfall methodology. What output should we expect? The answer is sustaining and increasing employee and customer satisfaction because this is vital for sustained growth. Agile marketing is also heavily dependent on the existing digital marketing plan, which is often absent in most marketing teams. We often perceive a marketing plan as a cocktail of tactics and channels without an overall strategy that integrates these marketing channels. The agile marketing plan focuses on the continuous improvement of customer acquisition, conversion and retention through various touch points and on all associated decision-making journeys that can exist within every customer touch point.

Direction and information

Prioritizing tactics is often ignored in marketing planning because of the lack of concrete insights as to which channels have the highest ROI. The input gained through customer insights and web analytics helps agile marketing teams to prioritize the highest-performing tactics, which also highlights that increased budget allocation to these channels is required. Marketing plans convey information about the budget allocation to different marketing channels and how these individual channels work together to achieve customer acquisition, engagement, conversion and retention. Having a plan, however, does not guarantee success in itself – a plan needs proper execution by skilled marketing teams. However, it's very easy to confuse tactics with a plan if there are no clear expectations of the KPIs and how they impact revenue streams.

Suppose you ask me what number of customer SEO is expected to be generated in the second quarter of the year; I would tell you to check the marketing plan. Without a marketing plan there is little or no agreement within the team about the expectation of each individual marketing channel as it relates to designated targets and objectives.

Customer insights

Agile marketing planning increases the likelihood of campaign success by integrating customer insights from web analytics and customer experience into the planning process. We all agree that there is a enormous difference between B2B and B2C marketing; yet research shows that some companies execute the same marketing strategy for both. Customer research that occurs during agile marketing planning generates the required insights for a well-informed marketing plan with the flexibility to adapt the plans to changes occurring during the course of the year. Suppose you are asked to estimate an increase of 20% in customer acquisition, engagement, conversion and retention across all marketing channels and how much it would cost, without wasting money on bad traffic. How possible would it be for you to estimate these metrics over a 12-month period, especially with the lack of control you have over external factors such as Google's algorithms and other technological innovations that constantly disrupt the industry? This is where agile is an absolute star, as it reduces uncertainty and enables you to make these predictions, albeit in short chunks of time (rather than the full year ahead).

Reducing uncertainty

Throughout the duration of a marketing plan, customer data is always available to the marketing team. The question is: how does marketing integrate internal data from internal teams (e.g. the call centre and customer experience team) which have direct contact and communication with new and existing customers? These teams, combined with web analytics and digital user experience, provide a rich source of new knowledge about customers, the technologies and touch points they use, as well as customer segments that are most profitable. It is critical that this rich source of customer insights be acknowledged and integrated into an ongoing agile marketing planning process, which is designed to help the marketing team to refine and restructure marketing channels and budget strategies. I think we can all agree that this approach to marketing planning is often ignored in marketing teams. Due to seasonality and other external factors, marketing channels and strategies that work well at the start of the year might not work as well at certain points during the year. Additionally, different customer segments will react differently to different marketing channels and strategies. From a cost-saving perspective, the channel with the highest ROI is hard to determine without the flexibility of adapting the budget to feedback generated from customer insights. An agile approach to marketing planning can greatly reduce the waste of budget on those marketing channels which are not effective enough.

A plan that contains a detailed forecast of marketing spend and outcomes for a period of 12 months is far from agile, because it lacks responsiveness. Most of us want - no, *need* - a marketing plan that responds to change informed by changing customer insights, as identified through analytics, CX and other relevant sources, and not according to the opinions of the highest-paid person in the room. How do we decide which channel or tactic to adopt to meet the overall business objectives that add value to shareholders and customers alike? Marketing plans help us to make cost-effective decisions about which channel and tactic would give the best marketing result at the lowest possible cost. Organizations need agile marketing in order to make decisions about how to respond to direct and indirect competitors in order to maintain and expand their market share. Sometimes companies create a marketing plan without a proper analysis of the competitor landscape, both existing and future one. For example, if a new start-up comes along that can produce a product or service that meets the needs of our customers at a cheaper cost, how would the marketing plan respond to this threat if there is no flexibility to cater for such events within the marketing plan? These scenarios are often not considered as part of the marketing planning process.

Often the best way to create and execute a marketing plan is to have all the customer insights needed at the start of the fiscal year with all the internal skills and expertise to execute the plan. Obviously, this is not always possible because of the multiple touch points and technology involved in marketing and the shortage of skilled T-shaped marketers required. This is why it is important to create an agile marketing plan that allows for flexibility in terms of regular and continuous updating of the plan on a weekly, monthly, or quarterly basis. It is also useful to identify trade-offs between channels that have been allocated funds from the budget, as well as the channels with the highest or lowest priority in the overall marketing plan. For example, a B2B marketing plan would focus heavily on educating and engaging customers because of the number of stakeholders involved in the purchase-decision process. The strategy for B2B, therefore, would tilt towards thought-leadership content creation and distribution with a heavy connection to the sales department of the organization in order to complete the purchase cycle from marketing-qualified leads to sales-qualified leads.

Team meetings

During my numerous conversations with Arie van Bennekum, one of the authors of the *Agile Manifesto*, he always emphasised that the success of agile is largely a result of the rituals, culture and team members' mindset that foster collaboration, open communication, and high visibility of everyone's tasks. We all have been in a meeting where there is a 'loudmouth' who completely takes over the meeting, limiting others from contributing their opinions or feedback. This can have a serious negative impact on the productiveness of the meeting and on the motivation of members within the team. In the interest of agile meetings staying short, to the point and providing every member an opportunity to share their progress, it's therefore important that the Head of Marketing (Scrum Master/Product Owner) has a pre-meeting conversation with the 'loudmouth' to request that they allow other members of the team to have their say. This section presents the different types of agile meetings, such as the sprint planning meeting, daily meeting, sprint review meeting, sprint retrospective, and backlog refinement, as well as some guidelines for making sure these meetings

are as effective as possible.

Sprint planning meeting

In agile marketing planning, there is no grand marketing plan that lasts 10 years, 5 years, or even 12 months, as we often hear about in most business organizations. Creating a multi-year marketing plan from a strategic level would have worked perfectly well before the Internet age but it would be risky to adopt such a mindset in today's marketing landscape. Depending on the size of your marketing team, industry and whether you operate in a B2B market, B2C market, or a combination of the two, you need to divide your marketing calendar into short sprints to allow for inspection and adaptation of the marketing plan to changing conditions in the marketplace.

Marketing planning and execution of iterations are time-boxed, meaning that we are focusing on a specific work stream that contains a number of agreed tasks. The marketing campaign calendar is split into four quarters of three-month periods with a budget allocated to each quarter according to channel and tactics. Agile marketing teams work in short time-boxed sprints of between one and four weeks, subject to what is agreed by team members. This allows for the overall marketing plan to be reviewed and adjusted regularly in relation to relevant and important market and customer insights gained from web analytics and customer-experience metrics during the sprint. The CMO reviews these insights and prioritizes the tasks for the next sprints to reflect the changes needed.

In the sprint planning meeting, the marketing plan is refined, so that tasks can be allocated into the four quarters of the year, which are then broken down into sprints. Channels and marketing strategies are refined into a thinly sliced task list for the sprints, then individual team members are assigned to each task. The sprint planning meeting could happen at the beginning of the week, fortnight, or month, depending on how you want to structure your sprints. The team meeting begins with an explanation from the CMO, or whoever else is the most senior member of the marketing team, of their vision and expectations from

Sprint planning meeting
Everyone gather together to create the task list for the week, month or quarter, depending on the context of your team. Every task must align with team and company objectives agreed for the quarter.

Web analytics | Customer experience   Objectives | Key results

the marketing team. Team objectives are set on a strategic level, to correlate to the overall business objectives and following this every individual within the team then creates and aligns their own individual objectives to the overall team objectives. During this meeting team members decide the amount of work they will complete for the next one, two or four weeks. It is important to encourage every member of the team to speak in these meetings because you cannot guarantee that everyone buys into the marketing strategy just because they fail to voice their concerns during planning meetings - everyone needs to be explicitly on board.

Appropriate representatives of each marketing speciality such as SEO, PPC, and offline advertising meet to discuss the marketing plan for the quarter. They then select items from the integrated marketing plan to include in the sprint plans for each channel team. For large marketing teams, each marketing channel then plans its own sprints while interacting with other team members in instances where dependencies exist. A good example of this is the interdependence between search engine optimization, paid advertising and social-media marketing, which all overlap and the planning of their activities requires a lot of communication and negotiation.

The outcome of each sprint goal must align with the overall marketing plan; each marketing team's sprint plan must highlight its dependencies on other teams to ensure proper understanding in terms of communication requirements between teams within the organization. Multinational marketing teams spread across different regions of the world would normally adopt a different agile marketing planning framework from that of smaller co-located marketing teams, which would require representatives from each region meeting frequently to identify dependencies between teams and marketing channels and working together to clarify their goals and responsibilities.

Daily meetings

The marketing team gather around the Kanban board every day, or a few days per week, depending on the way the team members decided to work together. The agile marketing team at Avaya.com meet once per week to discuss what each team member was working on the previous week, what they are working on in the current week, and what they plan to work on the following week. The team conversation also covers issues and obstacles hindering task completion of each team member which is then fed back to the Head of Marketing or

Daily meeting in front of the Kanban board (Task board)

TO-DO   DOING   DONE

Content Writer   Website Manager   Agile Coach

CMO   Digital Marketer

CMO, who can assist the team to remove these impediments.

To support quality and effectiveness, agile marketing teams should include no more than 9 people if everyone is going to be given chance to speak in team meetings. For teams of more than 9 people, it is important to break meetings into two groups. Small teams with less than 9 participants provide everyone with an opportunity to speak, although each member is encouraged to communicate their ideas succinctly in no more than 3 minutes. This means everyone must prepare a clear summary about the idea or information they wish to share in the meeting before attending. Meetings with larger audience sizes are considered more of an information broadcast (i.e. presentation), with only a few people allowed to ask questions at the end of the meeting, in the interest of keeping to time.

> *'Communication is the basic thread that ties us together. Through communication we make known our needs, our wants, our ideas, and our feelings. The better we are at communication, the more effective we are at achieving our hopes and dreams.'*
>
> *Alessandra & Hunsaker (1993)*

Review meetings

Review meetings are used by agile marketing teams to discuss campaign performance through an in-depth analysis of qualitative and quantitative analytics. During these meetings every member of the marketing team discusses and shares customer insights gained during the previous weeks.

Retrospective meetings

Esther Derby and Diana Larsen in their book *Agile Retrospectives* explain how retrospectives help agile teams to think and learn together in a participative and collaborative manner. The main purpose of retrospectives is to provide an overview of and feedback on each individual's performance and outcomes, as well as resolve any conflicts that may have arisen within the team throughout the sprint. These meetings are normally scheduled for the end of each sprint (every two weeks).

'The purpose of fostering constructive conflict is to have everyone put all their cards on the table, dissent, disagree, diverge, be 'ambiguous', be inconsistent with 'conventional wisdom' and be out in the open with their views or perspectives – regardless of their role, position, or place in the hierarchy. In an environment of constructive conflict, ideas can be refuted, disagreed with, countered, but cannot be silenced, cut off or shut down. There's a lot of noise, excitement, passion, and involvement – but nobody gets hurt.'

Peter G. Vajda

Different members of the team are assigned to facilitate retrospective meetings at the end of each sprint with the aim of discussing any areas of frustration experienced by team members during the recently completed sprint. These meetings help team members to talk about communication and interpersonal frictions that are causing stress within the team, with the aim of creating an environment which is psychologically safe. According to Henrik Kniberg, agile teams at Spotify believe retrospectives are special meetings because the team members are encouraged to review and adapt for continuous improvement. There are bound to be frictions and conflicts between team members for various reasons; any team that does not acknowledge and embrace conflict-resolution conversations in an open manner cannot become an agile marketing team. Retrospective meetings have a range of benefits to agile marketing teams, including:

> » Increasing and helping to improve listening skills across the team because everyone is encouraged to speak about whatever is on their mind;

> » Open communication across the team improves visibility and information sharing about marketing campaign performance so that everyone is updated with new information that might impact their role;

> » In situations where team members have conflicting goals, the conversations during retrospectives help team members

to reach reasonable compromises that result in win–win situations;

» For members of the team who are reticent about discussing whatever is bothering them, the retrospectives provide an opportunity for them to 'go direct' to discuss their issues for easy resolution;

» The open discussion and sharing of ideas across the team provide the platform needed for innovation to happen;

» They make team members feel valued because everyone on the team is treated equally.

» It is easier to reach an agreed decision about how to improve relationships moving forward.

As recommended by Derby and Larsen, it is important to update the team's working agreement during retrospective meetings to ensure that it aligns with changes within the team structure. Team members must communicate their concerns about their individual role and team issues to make everyone aware, while the Head of Marketing (Scrum Master/Product Owner) also asks team members tactical questions to understand how people feel about the performance of marketing campaigns during the last sprint. This line of questioning and the voluntary contributions from team members will lead to the development of a list of issues, obstacles and items that need improvements for the team to work on in the next sprint. It is important to highlight that during these meeting team members should avoid the mindset of blaming each other for issues that occurred during the sprint, but should instead work together to identify events causing problems for task completion. Once these have been identified and if they are external to the team, the Head of Marketing (Scrum Master/ Product Owner) should then work together with the relevant external stakeholders to make sure these are resolved, so that the marketing team can continue unhindered in the following sprint. Derby and Larsen also emphasise the importance of the Head of Marketing (Scrum Master/Product Owner) to remain neutral in all the discussions taking place amongst the team members, so that internal team dynamics is not negatively affected.

> *'Communication is the glue that holds an organisation together. The ability to communicate enables people to form and maintain personal relationships. And the quality of such relationships depends on the caliber of communication between people.'*

Dr Ruth Knight

Conclusion

As agile marketing teams we need to be careful about the notion that agile will help teams 'do twice the work in half the time'. The increased alignment, collaboration and team spirit agile offers marketing teams will be useless if the marketing strategy is only focused on increasing business revenue. The first step in successfully implementing agile (and reaping the benefits) is to create a customer feedback loop that informs the overall marketing strategy. Agile marketing should be focused on the context of each specific team. Teams should, therefore, avoid implementing 'Scrum by the book' and should feel free to mix elements of Scrum and Kanban as they are relevant to their specific circumstances. Some campaigns, like events, are waterfall in nature and a team can, indeed, integrate some of the agile rituals into waterfall type marketing campaigns. As an agile marketing professional you should feel free to research different type of frameworks and adopt or adapt whatever you feel will work best for your team. If you feel you need a more structured approach and some hand holding, you can always hire an agile coach with a broad experience of Scrum, Kanban and other frameworks, who will be able to work with you and your team and help you avoid some common pitfalls or first timer errors.

Chapter 5: Case Studies

Case Study One: Making Sales Agile

Contributed by Peter Eggleston, Sr.
Global Product Marketing Manager
at GE Healthcare

Background

An agile methodology promotes processes that are structured, adaptive and iterative, and encourages self-organization, teamwork and accountability. This makes agile methods well-suited for use in sales-focused organizations where the ability to adapt to fast-changing customer requirements and dynamic competitive environments is critical to effectively deploying and optimizing resources to achieve set financial targets. In this case study, we look at how a mid-tier enterprise software company brought an agile methodology into their sales process to effect a sales turnaround. The case study is based on a real company, but some details (including the name) have been changed on the request of the company's management team.

The company, which we will refer to as SoftCo, sold web development tools to mid-sized companies. Sales deals ranged from $50K to $200K, with an average deal size of $120K. Sales cycles ranged from 6 to 12 months and approximately 50% of the deals went through an RFP (competitive Request For Proposal stage). The sales team consisted of approximately a 1:3 ratio of inside tele-reps and regional field sales executives, which is a typical ratio in many enterprise sales organizations. SoftCo's inside team generated marketing qualified leads that were subsequently passed to the outside team for follow-up and completion.

SoftCo did well, growing at a modest pace for many years. However, as the market matured, they encountered increasing competition from many new companies and open-source platforms that put increasing pressure on their product features, functionality, as well as price. To address this issue, the company continued to invest in its development teams to keep the software modernized and competitive, but their market share eroded, as did their margins, since an increasing number of deals were done at lower price points to win the business. Unfortunately, SoftCo's sales revenue continued to slide and reached a point at which the company was no longer profitable and the size of the deals could not sustain the existing sales structure. The situation required a drastic intervention and a restructuring of both the sales team and the sales processes. SoftCo decided to reduce the outside sales force, grow the inside team, and at the same time bring both teams within an agile framework. The main aim of this was to gain more control and visibility over their opportunities and activities, so that these could be better managed to deliver more predictable pipeline conversion and increase the deal-conversion percentages.

Mapping agile onto the sales process

A good starting point for establishing a framework for applying agile principles to the commercialization process is to outline the key operational sales concepts, with a primary focus on: sales goals, sales stages (process), stage targets, pipeline volume and stage conversion.

'Standard' agile project management term	Agile sales equivalent
Epic	Sales goal
Project stage	Sales stage
Development tasks	Stage targets
Release	Pipeline volume
Software quality	Stage conversion

Sales goals are the revenue targets the organization is trying to achieve through selling its products or services. When applying agile principles, these agreed-on targets can be thought of as the 'sales epic'. That is, the end 'deliverable' is the amount of revenue that will be achieved as a result of the sales process over a given period of time. This corresponds to the software development definition of an epic, which is defined to be a set of functionalities that are delivered in one or more sprints, to then be put into production. When utilizing agile sales methodologies, quarterly sales targets are a good way to define your epics.

Once the epics have been determined, the next step is to gain an understanding of the *buying and selling process* that defines the sales stages. The artifact of this exercise is to segment these processes into a set of buying stages that indicate how your target customers discover their problems, search for solutions, evaluate these solutions and ultimately acquire products or services to solve their problems. Ideally, your company's sales process should map directly onto the consumer's buying process and this will then result in a well-defined set of steps in which the marketing and sales teams successfully engage your prospects. These processes, when executed, should lead to the prospects transitioning from one stage to the next in your sales pipeline. Most importantly, these events should be verifiable, which will lead to better accuracy in the sales forecasting.

The *stage targets* are quantifiable activities such the number of inbound leads, number of outbound calls per day, or other similar activity results (such as number of prospects qualified). It is important to have a good understanding of what the activity and results levels need to be in order to meet the desired sales goals. These will become the equivalent of development tasks: work that members of the agile team will perform to achieve the sales goals. However, one really powerful aspect of managing sales to an agile process is leveraging the concept of iterations (sprints) that support tweaking of the targets more rapidly than is possible to achieve in traditional sales organizations. This more rapid feedback supports better tracking and management of organizational activities so that the company's efforts will ultimately converge on the desired sales goal.

Sales organizations are well versed in producing *pipeline reports* for management reviews, and this fits nicely into the agile concept of a release. The time between the releases depends on the length of a product or service's typical sales cycle. Pipeline volume is simply the amount of suspects, prospects, deals, proposals, quotes, etc. in the various sales stages. The more closely you can tie the volume metrics to the sales outcome, the better you will be able to manage the process and predict your sales results.

Finally, *stage conversion* is a measurement of the amount of time it takes to move a customer from one sales stage to the next, and/or the percentage of customers converted to the next stage. You can think of stage conversion similar to software quality. It is a direct indicator of the quality and effectiveness of your sales processes.

Creating the backlog

As part of the turnaround, SoftCo decided to restructure the FTE deployment between inside and outside sales, inverting the ratio of inside to outside reps to 3:1. This was done partly to give an initial boost to filling the pipeline, as well as to reduce the cost of sales, as inside sales reps were paid approximately one third of the base salary of the outside, more-experienced enterprise sales team. The inside sales team generated leads through outbound methods such as cold calling and emails, as well as inbound activities consisting of call-ins, web forms and other inbound enquiries. A BANT (Budget, Authority, Needs, Timing) lead qualification process was implemented to ensure the quality of the leads before handover to the outside sales team. A lead was not deemed qualified unless three of the four BANT qualifiers were met.

These leads formed the user stories, as each lead had a problem they were trying to solve that was unique to them. The inside sales team documented these user stories during the several calls they had with the prospects in the qualification process. Once the user stories were developed for BANT-qualified leads, they were placed into the sales funnel. This funnel formed the backlog in the agile sales process. The outside sales team's goal was to develop the solution to the user story, 'burning down' the backlog to convert the leads in the funnel to sales.

An example of a sales user story would be: 'As a $450m on-line retailer of sporting goods, I have a $200m budget to modernize my eCommerce site and I need a tool that will allow me to redevelop it in four months, allow real-time inventory updates and on-line sales, and to be live before this year's holiday shopping season'.

Setting sprint iteration cycles for agile sales teams

In agile development, the epic is made up of a collection of user stories that is delivered over a series of sprints. Once SoftCo's inside team qualified and passed leads to the outside SoftCo sales team, they held regular sprint-definition meetings to discuss and prioritize which leads to actively pursue over a fixed time period, called a sales sprint.

In software product development, the sprint length should be long enough to produce something of value and demonstrability. If the sprint length is too short, one risks the possibility of not making meaningful progress between the sprints. However, if the interval is too long, then one may lose agility. While a sprint length of two weeks seems to be the universally adopted iteration length for software development teams utilizing agile development methodologies, SoftCo found that a one-week sales sprint cycle worked well. In fact, due to declining sales, SoftCo's upper management had implemented weekly pipeline reviews as a way to try to understand and apply more company brainpower to combat the waning sales and margins, so a weekly cadence was comfortable for the teams involved.

As the agile experiment progressed, SoftCo also found that the volume of prospects and customer activity they were now generating with the new inside sales team made a one-week interaction interval just right to keep on top of and react quickly enough to fast-moving sales opportunities and a more dynamic competitive sales environment. In a very dynamic and fast-paced commercial environment, one-day sprint intervals might be considered. However, in this case, Kanban might be a better methodology to consider.

Once the sales sprint iteration interval was decided on, SoftCo needed to define the makeup of the agile Scrum team – who would participate in the daily Scrum stand-ups and weekly sprint reviews. This involved considering what cross-departmental interaction was needed to more quickly and effectively engage the leads, and ultimately bring them through the sales funnel as quickly and optimally as possible to maximize the outside sales team's productivity.

Creating the agile sales team

Team composition in agile projects is typically cross-functional and self-organizing, and consists of the product owner, a customer representative and a mix of people doing the actual work. As discussed above, in a sales context we are defining the 'product' as the revenue resulting from the sale of one or more services or products. The sales team is essentially building and delivering a revenue pipeline. Therefore, in agile sales teams, the product owners could be regional sales managers in large companies, sales directors in mid-size organizations, or Vice-President (VP) of sales (or even the CEO) in small corporations. SoftCo, being a 250-person company, elected to make its Chief Commercial Officer the product owner, and its VP of Sales the Scrum master.

In most development organizations, a customer-facing representative such as a product marketing manager is responsible for communicating to the other team members what needs to be developed to solve customer problems. In agile sales, these individuals are the sales people or account managers, as being closest to the customer they hold the voice for what needs to be done to close each sales opportunity. One unique difference of applying an agile methodology to sales is that you will most likely end up with multiple customer representatives in the same sprint team (as a result of having multiple prospects in the pipeline and multiple salespeople or account managers responsible for collections of customers). One exception might be large-account sales where you have one team per customer, all servicing one single company. In practice, this is not a problem as all the sales members will have similar customer requirements and issues. Again, due to the size of SoftCo, one Scrum team was formed consisting of all the outside sales staff, called sales managers.

The remainder of the agile sales team was made up of the employees who were most often involved in supporting the sale. At SoftCo, this consisted of the department managers/leaders of employees with various departments could share knowledge and mentor one another. Everyone on the team learned from one another so that the impact of the sales team as a whole was greater than the sum of the contribution each sales manager might have made on their own in isolation. Meanwhile, having marketing, customer support and service as part of the Scrum team provided a quick and direct way for the internal teams to learn about customer needs and roadblocks to the sale. It also allowed the external sales teams to get 'just in time' knowledge about product features to support customer needs. This was a huge improvement over the previous method of sales training that consisted of product and marketing knowledge passed on once or twice a year. These tend to be arduous events with numerous slide decks, with the unfortunate consequence that much is forgotten due to the information overload associated with intense learning sessions.

The ability to change and adapt future plans based on current insights is a hallmark of agility, and the agile sales process gave SoftCo the agility it needed to outmaneuver its competition and reverse the direction of its sales. Improvements were seen within three months with a quicker pipeline conversion, higher opportunity win rate, and renewed spirit of optimism across the entire company. In fact, the newly slimmed-down outside sales teams closed as many deals as the three-times-larger sales team that preceded it. The company is now once again commercially viable and growing.

Case Study Two: Scrum Application in a Creative Services Group

Contributed by Julee Bellomo,
Enterprise Agile Consultant

agile process themselves.

» The Director facilitated a planning meeting where the business people brought all their requests to be prioritized against each other. This eliminated the need for team members to determine which request was most important. Instead, they made the entire backlog transparent, which helped create trust on the business side and eliminate 'pet' projects.

» The organization invested in hiring a coach to help with evangelizing and training Scrum in within the team as well as the wider business.

» We created business agility – a balance between iterative creating work, responding to change, and delivering on time. First, we established the Scrum framework to create a cadence of predictable delivery and ability to respond to change. In this team, since there was no established product owner, the Director acted as the Chief Product Owner, who was the ultimate decision maker. For a short time, the coach helped facilitate the Scrum process. In this group, there was a team member who had the personality, desire, and interest to become the Scrum Master, and the business helped support this evolution of his role. We felt that a one-week sprint would help us manage the very fluid backlog and keep our forecasts realistic. In order to highlight the best of the Scrum framework with this shared, specialty team, we established two specific practices.

» We established a rank-ordered list of priorities by the business. The Director acted as the facilitator for a priority meeting with representatives from all divisions, several days before the sprint started. The biggest change was to support the Scrum value of working on the highest-value requests, not date-driven requests.

» We broadened the definition of 'done'. Every opportunity the team had where they could help the business make a decision, a definition of done was created. This took planning and commitment from both the business and the team. The dialogue in non-IT teams can sound much different from how it does if we are forecasting the work to complete a finished software feature.

'I'd like to deliver the second draft to you by the end of next week. In order to do this, if I can get you a design by Thursday, can you commit to a response by Monday?'

In retrospect

From a manager: 'You often hear how agile doesn't work for designers, but I think we did a great job at taking the bigger projects and breaking them down into the digestible chunks that were manageable. This helped us do a good job at managing scope creep as well'.

We created a learning organization because agile maturity takes time. In the first quarter, we focused on getting things done and establishing trust, not metrics. In the second quarter, we established a Scrum Master who could help facilitate the process, the relationships, and the goals. By the third quarter, we had started to focus on closing the gap between UX testing and development. We also had some useful metrics from the tool we were using, which helped us analyze trends, such as the type of work, and the biggest customers. Surprisingly, the data told us that the divisions with the most valuable requests were different from what was perceived when we started. The data also made it very transparent as to the type of skill sets we needed to hire for because of the shift from print media to electronic media.

We can now celebrate! Agile creates lots of changes to celebrate and our company was able to capitalize on the success not just in outward accomplishments, but intrinsic value as well.

Prepare for the journey

A transformation, by definition, requires change, so be prepared to work through the resistance and not give in to challenges and hybrid solutions to Scrum. Early on in this engagement, business customers started 'bargaining', such as a request to split the percentage of time available across all divisions, for example: to split capacity to serve Sales 30% of the time, Marketing 30% of the time, etc. Our response was to continue to communicate that the team was working on value-driven requests, not date-driven requests. The leaders backed up the team by:

> » being willing to pay a fee for late deadlines to publications in order to support team working on a large conference deadline;

> » being willing to outsource lower-priority items that had an established brand, such as point-of-sale items and conference collateral.

> » getting buy-in: taking the time to create and communicate the vision, and to get others involved in the decision making.

In retrospect

A quote from the Creative Services Manager in this case study:

> » 'I think it was very important that we had the buy-in to set the priorities because if we didn't have that, it wouldn't work. The other very important aspect is that it made the team accountable for what they agreed to. I tried implementing some of what we did at my new company and it didn't work because the buy-in wasn't there'.

Going back to the three goals we established before embarking on this transformation, we are confident in declaring a success in:

> » improving the flow of work in Creative Services

From the Director of Communications: 'It has now become the way work gets done with the creative services team. It laid the foundation to transform how work flows through the team. There's a lot more collaboration and transparency than there was before'.

> » reducing interruptions and creating a more sustainable pace – interruptions were 15% or less.

From a business customer:

> *'It was surprising how the interruptions started to decrease as we started to establish trust'.*

> » mitigating individual silos and increasing team competencies

One of the graphic artists commented, just three months into the agile transformation:

> *'It has changed my life. I no longer dread coming into work'.*

Case Study Three: Agile Beyond Software Development - Application in Human Resources

Contributed by Emma Sharrock,
Author of The Agile Project Manager

Introduction

I was working in a digital company of 650 employees, implementing agile ways of working for software delivery teams. We had started a pilot, and had situated the team on a different floor from the other delivery teams. The team adapted well to collaborating on a daily basis, visual management and the new ceremonies of agile. In fact, the organisation outside Technology started to adapt too: they became very curious. I communicated regularly with the wider organisation through blog posts and emails to technology and non-technology teams who were identified as impacted by the changes we were implementing. The communications always welcomed people to observe our stand-ups and showcases, and, of course, come up any time to ask questions.

The HR team was especially interested, mainly because their work area was right next to the pilot teams, and also the Director of HR was very interested in the benefits that increased collaboration can bring to employee well-being. She asked whether I could help them implement some agile practices. The HR team was already highly collaborative, communicating openly on a daily basis, but they knew that with some tools, techniques and coaching they could improve.

The process

I started with a workshop where we identified the high-level goals of HR, including what it would mean to them and the wider organisation when these were achieved. I find this an essential part of the planning process, because when a team can identify with something bigger than themselves, they are so much more connected to their goals. Once the team was clear on where they were going, we spent some time breaking down the goals into smaller pieces of work. We did breakouts with the sub-teams and each sub-team came up with their individual 'stories' that contributed to the overall goals. We then spent some time breaking down the first quarter of the year into more detailed tasks.

I asked them how they would like to visually manage their work. Up until that point, their only exposure to visual management had been the software delivery team, and they were working in two-week sprints. They were reluctant to work like that as their tasks, even though they had been broken down, were still too high-level to work at such a cadence. We discussed whether time boxing would be useful to them, and they agreed it would and they were happy to manage their goals on a quarterly basis. So they designed a Kanban board with all their goals for the year in a backlog, with detailed tasks for Quarter One in 'To Do'. I facilitated the first couple of stand-up meetings where they shared their priorities and progress and they agreed to continue with stand-ups twice a week.

Key learnings

Minimise the work in progress. The tam realized quickly that they had a lot going on all at once. Whenever a card was moved from 'To Do' to 'Doing', I asked if there was anything in 'Doing' that could be finished first. This raised awareness to the importance of finishing wherever possible before starting new things. This in turn avoided too much context switching across multiple tasks.

Visual management can be exposing, but that's okay. Many team members were not used to being so open about their work in the past. Deep down we all experience a bit of 'impostor syndrome' and fear about how others might perceive us. Creating a trusting environment was really important to make people feel safe to open up and share what they were doing. This came from supportive leadership (who also shared what they were doing) and gentle reminders to listen without judgement and support each other.

Discover duplication. When all their work was more visible, it became clear that there had been quite a bit of duplication of effort. People were doubling up on work that could easily be done by one person. Catching this early saved heaps of time and potential angst.

Helping each other. Ideally, no team has a single point of failure, but sometimes this happens. When the team started to share more of their work with each other, they identified opportunities to help each other. When someone's work was piling up due to overload or issues with getting external help, support or sign-off, this was immediately obvious visually and through the stand-up discussion. This opened up opportunities for team members to assist each other.

Learning. When work is represented visually and talked about more often, opportunities for learning present themselves. As well as overload issues coming to light, so do opportunities for a team member to shadow another person while they work, and in turn learn from the experience. Many teams can fall into the trap of always giving certain work to the same people equipped with the skills needed, thus creating a constant dependence on that person. A team should (of course) be delivering for business value, but also ensuring in every sprint there are deliveries for learning. This is a win/win, as people who are learning and being challenged are more satisfied at work, AND by learning, you gradually remove key-man risks and bottlenecks.

Conclusion

Some compare agile to a virus that is introduced into an organisation. That organisation has a certain amount of 'immunity' or resistance to the change. Sometimes there is so much 'immunity' or resistance that agile cannot get a foothold and dies out just like a virus does in a healthy person. Introducing agile into a number of areas, especially with highly motivated teams willing to do things differently and learn through the process, means you can create positive stories around the change that are likely to quickly spread within the wider organisation. Good news and bad news travel quickly, so those positive stories play a really important role in breaking down the resistance in areas that may have had negative experiences in agile (from within or outside the organisation). HR and other support teams are great places to start an organisation's agile transformation to help build momentum for change, role-model behaviours and support for the wider organisation as they in turn take on the change.

Case Study Four: Agile Marketing at Avaya.com

Contributed by Michael McKinnon, Global Marketing Operations at Avaya.com

My agile marketing journey started back in 2009. At the time one of our clients was a company called Rally Software and on one of my visits with the client I learnt about agile methodology. When we started agile, it was all about 'sticky notes' on a giant office board – just numerous sticky notes in different colours all over the wall. We had the old-fashioned system of four columns to group the sticky notes into:

» To do

» Doing

» In progress

» Done.

After a while, we modernized and moved to using Kanban software boards such as Jira and Kanbanize.

I look at agile as 'a way to get sh** done'; that's exactly what it is. Agile marketing is the way to manage team productivity and efficiency. It helps us get stuff done as quickly as possible, get the solutions out and get feedback on them in order to make them better. However you choose to do that, whichever processes and/or frameworks you employ, it is simply a way to get stuff done. Agile is about putting minimal processes around getting things done in order to get a marketing task completed.

Using agile methodologies in a marketing context, I created, replicated, streamlined and improved processes to reach our planned goals. The process focused on lead routing, lead scoring, lead nurturing, campaign hierarchy and campaign execution. Agile in marketing is about helping you get stuff done and managing your team in such a way that they all feel as if they are moving forward, individually and as a team. It is about breaking down silos within the marketing team and the organisation in general in order to use the existing synergies to make your work more productive and more efficient.

My team was too big for daily scrum (stand-up) meetings, so instead we did them weekly. These meetings provide a forum for the broader team to discuss issues and problems they might be having with whatever tasks they are working on. I see the following benefits in agile:

Breaking down the silos between the marketing and other departments within the organisation: agile gives increased organisational visibility to your team's activities and goals. When someone comes to your team saying: 'Hey, I need this done', you can show them your board with details of your schedules for the week, month and/or quarter. You can then ask them where they think their work fits into the marketing team's schedule towards the broader organisational goal. If I input your work into my Kanban (to-do list), that means I have to remove something else from my list of things to do. Then the conversation is no longer based on marketing teams making a decision based on personal preferences, saying: 'I like you so I am going to do your project and I am really not going to tell this other guy that his project is being delayed because I decided to do yours first, even though I had him on my to-do list earlier. Oh and, by the way, he is never going to know'. Agile marketing takes away the uncomfortable decisions when it comes to external requests coming into the marketing team, because it brings visibility to the conversation about how the marketing team prioritises work. Allowing everyone to see requests coming into the marketing team and how these tasks are ranked and allocated, based on their impact on the bottom line, is crucial in agile. This means that individuals are no longer in charge of the decision making with regard to what task to complete because all decisions are based on what's best for the company – as opposed to prioritising work based on who you like or any other personal favours that are happening in the background.

Agile helps to integrate new members into the team immediately so that onboarding happens really quickly because all new team members can see and access the Kanban board. This gives them a view of what everyone on the team is doing and how different tasks align towards a shared objective; the new employee immediately sees how they fit into the existing system. They are also able to see what they are doing and how that fits into everything else within the team. In non-agile teams, when a new employee arrives, we sit them down and give them a list of tasks they are expected to complete at the end of the first month and they basically have no idea how the task they will be doing in the first month is contributing to the organisation. Without proper induction, new employees don't see the big picture until well after six months into their role.

Agile helps all team members understand how their role relates to the big picture. Our agile marketing iterations are done quarterly with a full list of everything that needs to be done for each quarter. The next step is to break it down into tasks and assign these tasks to individuals within the team. Then each team member starts moving the task through the typical Kanban flow from 'in progress' to 'doing', 'blocked' and then 'done'. Everyone can see how the task flows and the interdependencies between all the tasks on the board, which makes it clear how each individual task contributes to the organisation as a whole. The Kanban flow is simply a way to visualise and free roadblocks to task completion caused by external and internal dependencies.

When I came to Avaya, my team consisted of 15 people spread across the world, in India, Argentina, California, New Jersey and Germany. Because my team members were not located in the same office we decided to work with a virtual Kanban board as it was easier to get up and running. I started with team members by saying: 'OK, let's just meet once every two weeks'. First of all, I trained the entire team about agile marketing by delivering a presentation to explain the agile values and principles. This was easy for my team to understand because marketing people tend to be pretty technology-savvy compared to a sales team who can sometimes (although not always) be almost like dinosaurs in terms of technology. We all agree that sales teams hate any technology that gets in their way and much prefer the face-to-face human interaction and this is fair enough, as customers want to feel they are talking to a human being in order to close the deal. Marketing people, on the other hand, often work in the background, paving the way for sales, which - today - requires being well-versed in all aspects of tech.

My team and I agreed that if any member of the team got a task request from within or outside the team we would not write the task down on a piece of paper (notebook). Instead, we would update it into the online Kanban board. Every two weeks the whole team met to review everyone's task list on the Kanban board. We reviewed linked tasks and projects to identify any duplicate tasks and we also grouped similar tasks and then slowly built them into larger projects. This was a gradual process that lasted over three months to get everyone thinking about working with the Kanban board and reviewing and prioritising tasks. As the marketing team leader, it took me about four months to be able to channel all team communication through our online Kanban board. This allowed us to reduce our email communications to the absolute minimum. Some members of the team adapted to use virtual Kanban boards and some took a little longer, but now everyone in my team responds to my questions via the Kanban board. That's what we wanted as a team, a central place for all communication and tasks to avoid communication via an endless chain of emails that usually results in vital information being lost or buried. This was the first stage of the agile marketing process, which was my way to get everyone familiar with using a virtual Kanban board.

The next step was arranging our meeting once every quarter for iteration planning. We aimed to use our virtual Kanban board as a strategy-planning tool and these meetings lasted between one and two hours. After each member's strategic priority had been assigned, they would break it down into specific objectives, such as:

> » I need redo the email lead routing.

> » I need to build nurture tracking for the contact centre business unit.

> » I need to redo campaign hierarchy so that the campaign team can execute and get reporting better.

Once the objectives are defined, we ask ourselves the question: What are the tactics required to achieve these objectives? Then we lay out the list of tactics. We also allow a 3-hour block every week for each team member to be able to deal with whatever external task comes through to them – the random unexpected requests that other people will often throw your way at work, without any regard for your work plan. The team continued to use the virtual Kanban board to manage external tasks from other departments, as well as to maintain task visibility across the teams.

We used the first quarter of the year as a bottom-up approach to agile, and the second quarter as a top-down approach to our agile marketing adoption. For the second quarter, we started getting the way it should be: through objective setting, followed by task allocation arising from each objective, before moving the tactics through the agile methodology. That's where we are now because we meet every quarter, agree our objectives, mark out the marketing tactics for each objective, break them down into tasks and distribute these to different members within the team. We also try to estimate the time that each task will take so that we have an idea how long each team member will be spending on this and plan their capacity to complete the task. Depending on job role, everyone has about 5 to 15 hours per week to do something else that might come onto their to-do list apart from the regular tasks allocated to them on the Kanban board. We still meet each week to go over what got done in that week, what our individual blockers are and what we plan to do the following week. Everyone has 10 minutes to talk about these three points because we meet only once per week as opposed to having a daily stand-up meeting (as recommended by scrum). As the leader of the team, I am responsible for removing the impediments that block my team from completing their tasks. Oftentimes these impediments are completely unrelated to our work and come from external teams. It's very easy for other business units to ignore requests from marketing teams and it's my duty as the marketing scrum master to ensure that these political issues are resolved in order to avoid delays.

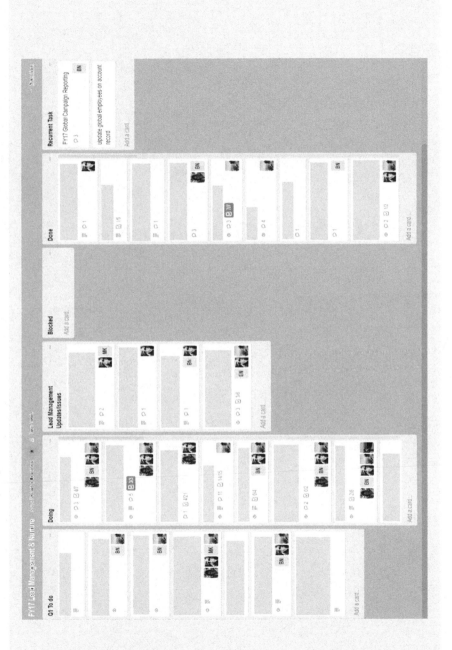

Case Study Five: Agile in Cross-Functional Teams

Contributed by Mia Kolmodin, Agile Coach, Product Management

Towards the end of 2016 I wrote a post titled 'Agile in a Nutshell' for my agile basics coaching for teams or students. The posting has now become something of an Internet phenomenon with over 6,000 likes on LinkedIn, and over 3,000 shares. When Femi [Olajiga, the author] contacted me to ask me to write a piece for his book on agile for marketing, it was because he had seen this post. I'm an Agilist with a background in graphic design and previous experience as an art director, but I am now doing agile coaching mostly on product ownership and user experience, helping teams and organizations to become better at meeting the agile requirements utilizing Lean UX and working in cross-functional teams with continuous discovery and delivery. My work is most fun when the team owns the 'what' and the 'how', co-creating and delivering together. However, it didn't always use to be this way. The story I would like to tell is about my start in Agile and Lean UX.

Having had my daughter in 2003, I went back to work two years later, in 2005, at a company working with lead generation websites driving traffic purely on SEO. I stayed at this company for five years, mainly because I learned so much new stuff and worked with truly skilled and nice people. When I started there, it was as an art director assigned with a website to 'design'. I asked who the target audience was and what the goal of the site was. I also wanted to know whether there was someone I could work with who already knew the target audience, and perhaps a developer. This company, like so many others, was organized in functional teams where people with the same competence were working side by side, even though they had different projects. It was not an easy thing to design a good website in these conditions, since I had to come up with everything, from information architecture and wireframes to graphic design with logotype – and all this within only a week or two. When I was done with my work, I handed it over to the project manager, who sat on it until the developers were ready to start working on it, which could sometimes be a long as months later. This always seemed to me to be a very inefficient, and an utterly uncreative way of getting things done.

After about a year at this company, one of the developers told me he thought my design was really difficult, and that it took several extra weeks to code the last e-shop because of the opacity of the boxes. I could not believe what I was hearing; had he really been sitting for several weeks, working on it and being angry with me, without even bothering to walk across the office and talk to me about it? He got a really long face when I told him the opacity was there simply because it was the fastest way for me to set the correct colour in Photoshop with the keypad. This was the tipping point for me and I started to research different ways of managing web projects without hand-offs. I found Agile and Scrum, which seemed to be much better ways of working. I went and talked to my developing manager and said I thought it would be a great thing if we could start working agile with Scrum instead, that it would probably make us several hundred per cent more efficient, with higher-quality solutions, as well as making working together much more fun. After a few weeks, when nothing happened, I spoke to my CEO instead, telling him the story about the misunderstanding costing several weeks of unnecessary work and how much we could probably save. He became very interested, and said he would look into it right away. This was just before the summer vacation and, when I got back, my CTO had been fired, and the CEO asked me whether I would be interested in the position and implementing Scrum? I turned the offer down since I thought I had enough on my plate already – with a small child and as the only designer in a company of about 150 people. However, this was the starting point of our joint Agile journey. We started the Agile transformation by bringing in an Agile coach from Crisp, who is one of my colleagues today. I joined one of the new Scrum teams, and we hired some more designers for the other teams as well. Everyone who wanted could do the Scrum Master training, and we had between two and four Scrum Masters in each team, rotating every third sprint. These were fun times! We learned a lot and became really strong as teams counting story points and looking for process improvements everywhere.

As a designer, I had one specific problem with Scrum: should I work one sprint ahead of the developers, or in the same sprint being stressed as hell to be able to deliver? I talked a lot about this with our Agile coach, and we tried both. As I wanted to sit in with the team and work with them, rather than serving them, I worked in the same two-week sprint, on the same stuff, ending up doing less overhead and hand-offs, with more pair designing between me and the front-end developer. It went really well, and I was also being Scrum Master for some of the sprints, really enjoying the agile ways of working.

After a year or so working with Agile, I started to work in a team doing only conversion optimization. We were a team of three web analytics professionals, one back-end developer, one front-end developer, and me as an art director. We worked on landing pages and websites. We started to work in Kanban instead of Scrum, but still doing retrospectives every two weeks to improve on our process as much as possible. We became really strong working as a team, almost like a machine. We started out by identifying what site or landing page had the most traffic but lowest conversion rate, creating our hypotheses together based on a conversion framework; doing it the same way every time as a team made it easy to improve the method as well. After creating one or two hypotheses, we did one or two first-draft wireframes together on our whiteboard; after that, I created the graphic design and the front-end developer started to code it. We always tried to challenge the old approach to optimization to see how much we could improve the framework we had developed for landing pages, review pages and so on. It was always exciting to see the results after two business weeks; sometimes we were right in our hypotheses and we could see big improvements. What you learn the most, though, is that much of the time you are wrong in your assumptions and, best of all, that it doesn't matter whether you are the highest-paid person or not, your ideas aren't necessarily the best ones out there.

Some designers claim it is not possible to work in an agile setting in a good way. I strongly disagree: it is a perfect set-up with short feedback loops perfect for user research and design, making it possible to learn quickly what works or doesn't work. With a Lean UX approach, instead of the moldy old backlog created by only one person, containing a never-validated hypothesis, the team can gain valuable insights and act directly without any need for micromanagement. All that management needs to do is to give the team time to stabilize and mature as a team, to develop a mandate in the team to make business decisions as they go along, and to include the right competences within the team. If they need, for example, web analytics professionals or designers to do their work effectively, these should be included in the team, not in a function-specific support team. I have never seen this work without this set-up; as soon as you leave any of these parameters out, the magic is gone and you can't get high-performing teams delivering both the right thing and at speed. The team should be able to work together on the same prioritized things, knowing exactly what the business goal is, working and using the most lean methods and process possible. Never have reporting or documenting as a main goal; it should always be the lessons learned, the releasable features and creating the biggest possible user and business value that are considered the most important achievement for the whole team. It also shouldn't matter who in the team does what, the team should decide this based on their internal makeup and the task at hand. The best possible set-up, in my mind, is to take away the different titles and just go with 'team member' as each individual's title, to build equity within the team, whilst working really hard to understand the specific competences your team members have and utilizing those as much as possible to work together and learn from each other.

This is my special recipe for a superior agile set-up in cross-functional teams, creating sustainable and happy teams that love their work, are able to deliver value, make their own decisions and evolve both as individuals and as team members. On top of this, it also rewards the business with strong and fast results, which improve its bottom line - a complete win-win!

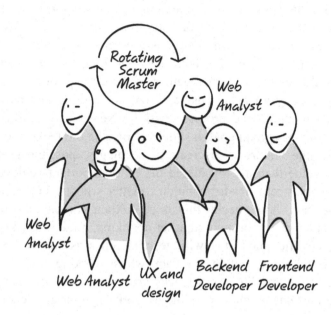

Team Kanban Board

Case Study Six: In-flight Program Transformation Using Kanban

Contributed by Sam Zawadi, Lean Agile Change, Delivery, Transformation – Consultant and Trainer

Background

A Project Management Office (PMO) transformation team was needed to engage a large business and IT change program worth tens of millions of pounds. The program had been running for almost a year, and targets were not being achieved. The problem was further compounded by fragmented and inconsistent ways of working employed across the program and within the PMO itself. This made it difficult to identify problems and to address them in a prioritised manner, understand what each PMO team member was actually working on, whether they were working on the right things at the right time, visualise our work as a team and stop overloading work onto the team.

Our goals

Our goals were:

> » To transform the existing PMO into a service that adds value to the wider portfolio;

> » To address the pain points of the business and IT change program through the PMO transformation.

My team set about achieving these goals within an agreed time frame and budget.

Running the PMO transformation

Before we could begin to address the problem areas of the in-flight program, we had to get our own ducks in order. We built a transformation plan to raise the level of PMO service available to the in-flight program, and to prepare the PMO to serve the rest of the business portfolio. We found that the key program problem areas were directly linked to an underperforming PMO, so transforming the PMO directly impacted the operation of the program, adding more clarity and better reporting metrics – an all-round positive achievement.

We built a small transformation team of five experienced project and program experts. Each team member was highly skilled and had an expertise that was directly related to a program issue. The team was therefore made up of the following:

» An expert in risk and issue management;

» An expert in project and program reporting and communications;

» An expert in governance and control;

» An expert in program planning and dependency management;

» An expert in project delivery and leadership.

It should be noted that whilst each team member had their speciality, they were also well versed in other project portfolio management (PPM) practices; this ensured that we built a T-shaped team that was able to deal with differing incoming queries and requests.

First things first, we had to understand where our work was coming from, and how we could best prioritise that work in order to meet the needs from across the program – we needed someone who would take ownership of and prioritise our backlog. We identified this person as the PMO Manager who had a direct interface to the Program Director. We worked with the PMO Manager on a daily basis in reviewing and prioritising our backlog. If there were difficult prioritisation discussions to be had, we could rely on her to make those calls, with our support. This left our team free to get on with their work and assured all of us that we were working on the right thing at the right time.

Our ways of working

In order to meet the demand at a consistent pace, we employed a lean and pragmatic approach to regulating and tracking our work. Real-world problems need to be fixed with 'doers' (operators) rather than 'thinkers' (consultants); therefore, we actively reached out to all facets of the program, captured as many requirements as we could into a single backlog of work, and then we visualised our work on a physical board. We used the Kanban method to run the PMO transformation. Visualising our work on a physical board not only served the team well in terms of prioritising our work and limiting our WIP (work in progress), but it also gave us a team presence within the business, working alongside other business teams to help the program deliver its objectives. This proved to be a powerful visual statement and learning point across the business.

The Kanban method we introduced resulted in better resource planning, and enabled us to continuously work alongside the program to ensure we were fully aligned against its needs and the future vision for the PMO. Once a 'PMO heartbeat' was established, personnel from other areas of the business learnt how we ran the transformation teams, and applied what they learnt to their own teams. Through our doing, we were also educating, and the level of value-addition we offered as a team quickly became apparent.

Establishing our workflow

We built our Kanban board by spending around three hours in a workshop documenting what our workflow is for the kind of work we do. For example, our goals were to provide a service as well as deliver a PMO transformation, which included work such as reviewing and simplifying the program governance processes, defining a better quality management approach, understanding and documenting how program finances are tracked and managed, creating supporting program documentation, addressing program pain points, risks, issues, etc.

We mapped out our workflow based on demand; initially, most of the demand came from producing program assets such as better supporting processes for risk management and aspects of agile and waterfall governance. We used post-its and laid them out horizontally to simulate steps in our Kanban workflow, so that we could easily discuss and change them around if we needed to. We identified the following initial workflow:

Backlog --> Doing --> In review --> Implementing --> Done.

Our next step was to understand firstly when we are able to start a piece of work, and call this our *definition of ready* (DoR). Our DoR statement comprised a checklist of statements that would have to be true in order for us to be able to start on a piece of work; if the answers were all true, that meant we had a green light for starting the work. For example:

1.   Has this item been prioritised by the PMO Manager?

2.   Have the requirements been clarified and understood (including any deadline requirements)?

3.   Do we have the skills in the PMO to be able to do this work?

Once our DoR was established, we needed to understand when we could formally say that work was done, so we agreed on what 'done' looked like for us. Because of the nature of our work, the two key aspects that went into our *definition of done* (DoD) were the creation of the document or process itself AND the successful implementation of the document or process into the program – in other words, creation of the asset and acceptance by the program. This gave us the responsibility of not only process improvement, but also implementation and establishment of that process into the program ecosystem. If all the following conditions were true, this meant we were truly done with our work items:

1.   Has the work been completed within the PMO?

2.   Has it been reviewed and signed off internally in the PMO?

3.   Has the work been implemented in the program?

4.   Has the work been accepted and signed off by the relevant program area?

Now that we had both a DoR and a DoD, we had to think about our capacity as a team. Given that the team was new to using a Kanban approach, we decided to start simple. We printed out avatars for each team member, and each team member was given only two avatars. This meant that they could only ever have two avatars each on the board at any one time. This helped to narrow focus, mitigate against excessive context switching, and regulate the flow of work across our board. We started with two as an arbitrary number that felt right for us.

Finally, due to further thinking and discussion that took place by generating both our DoR and our DoD, we decided to amend our workflow to better reflect our reality, so we wrote up the following amended workflow on a physical board, adding the two additional steps of 'Clarifying requirements' and 'Assessing for go/no go':

Prioritised Backlog --> Clarifying requirements --> Assessing for go/no go --> Doing --> In review --> Implementing --> Done.

As a side note, we decided to use verbs to name each state of the workflow, because for us this indicated activity and action, which we found more encouraging.

A light process

Now that we had built our new Kanban board, we had daily stand-ups and we walked the board from right to left, highlighting issues and impediments as we did our updates. The PMO Manager was usually part of our stand-ups, which was useful because many impediments we faced could usually be resolved by escalating for a priority call or a clarification of the specific requirement we had to meet. We had retrospectives when we felt there was a need, however, we found ourselves doing retrospectives approximately once per month, which suited our rhythm and ways of working.

Conclusion

The result of our efforts was a full-service PMO that was able to respond to the program's needs more effectively, more quickly, and based on a balanced and agreed backlog priority, which meant that we were able to address the right program needs at the right time, as well as visualise our work and understand our team's work in progress limits. We continued to operate this way and inspect and adapt our workflow, and experiment with our WIP limits and we soon had representatives from other areas of the program and business attending our stand-ups as curious bystanders, asking questions about our methods, how the board works, etc. Our ways of working were starting to spread. New reporting structures, reporting metrics, governance models, change control processes, program planning support, risk management processes, documentation templates, etc. were established into the program over a period of time (which we called the Phase 1 Transformation). Overall, the PMO Transformation was seen as a success and an example of how agile methods can work not only for software development teams, but also for any team that needed to be able to visualise their work and respond to changing priorities on a regular basis.

Case Study Seven: Applying the Principles of Lean and Kanban to Hack the Common Problems of Marketing Teams

Contributed by Monica Georgieff, Head of Marketing at Kanbanize

Recent studies conducted by the American Marketing Association show that almost all marketing teams, no matter their size, face similar challenges. Marketing managers name the following as the toughest obstacles to overcome in order to be optimally efficient and effective in their teams:

» lack of communication;

» lack of experienced staff;

» lack of reporting;

» lack of financial resources (budget).

Most modern marketing professionals rely on a combination of CRM tools, copious Excel charts, digital calendars and physical notebooks in order to stay organized. However, they end up neglecting to structure, manage and improve their actual workflow – the stream of daily tasks that their team members undertake in order to deliver value to their customers. Tracking tasks from initiation to completion in a way that allows the collection of data from the process as a whole can be beneficial to a marketing team in several ways. It can help them track cost in relation to other metrics, report to each other, their customers and to higher management, as well as nurture knowledge sharing and continuous improvement.

The principles of the Lean and Agile methodologies are tried and tested approaches to making the best of one's resources using a disciplined and predictable flow of work. Over the last 50 years, the methods of their application, Kanban and Scrum, have worked wonders for both the manufacturing and IT industries. By mapping workflow on a Kanban board, for example, marketers could effectively tackle the scattering of information, the waste of valuable resources, and the miscommunication within their teams.

As Lean and Agile methodologies remain relatively unexplored in the creative space, marketing professionals have not yet fully embraced them as viable solutions to the challenges that exist in the marketing space. This oversight translates into a deepening of the existing problems that prevent teams in this field from continually improving their efficiency and working waste-free.

Adopting Lean principles and Kanban workflow management in marketing

I had never heard of Kanban before I was brought in by the CEO of Kanbanize to work with the founding team to put together a 'mean, Lean marketing machine'. I was aware of the typical problems marketing teams often have to tackle, so I was curious to see if the Lean approach would help the team prevent any of these.

The SaaS marketing team was, at the time, dealing with a lack of experienced personnel and a lack of a definitive structure of its processes. Furthermore, as a relatively young company, we could not afford to waste any of our resources, such as time and budget, on whims. At the same time, between the team members we were generating a growing list of ideas that required some type of workflow if they were to ever get executed. Together, we would need to conserve our time resource, meaning that we would need to be fast; we would need to compete with companies that already ran established campaigns in our value network; we would need to be effective; we would need to allocate funds only to high-impact campaigns we could track and we would need to be efficient.

We decided to initially focus on acting on the ideas that complied with the first principle of Lean: value. As a team policy, we decided we would only work on the ideas for which we saw demand in our value network and we addressed the users who could use our SaaS product to solve a particular set of problems. In other words, we eliminated ideas that would not target our value networks directly, or that we could not validate; anything under the vague, but familiar, hat of 'brand awareness': things such as billboards, ads 'in fun' instead of professional social media, and pamphlets – all these had to go.

To tackle the challenge of structuring our process and creating a pipeline for our measurable campaigns and the tasks associated with them, we decided to explore a Kanban implementation of Lean. Although most creative teams experimenting with Kanban begin working on physical Kanban boards, using post-it notes, we started with a digital Kanban board made in Kanbanize. We believed the visual nature of the method as well as the ability to generate reports, monitor analytics and track efficiency online would help us with continuous improvement of our process. We considered it an investment for the future as our team grew and our campaigns became more sophisticated.

There were three (and logistically even more) very obvious disadvantages to the physical Kanban board that we foresaw from the get-go:

» we were not able to collect much data from the board manually;

» we noticed that it was excluding remote team members who were not based on site at the company office;

» we anticipated that managing the whiteboard with papers would get crowded and might end up even more chaotic.

We were hoping a digital Kanban board would mean that we could:

» include our remote team members as users on the board and effectively collaborate on projects we were running together;

» have access to our boards on-the-go through Android and iOS apps;

» get detailed analytics about our process and define areas of improvement;

» generate internal reports using specific data collected over the course of the work process;

» potentially automate parts of our process so we wouldn't spend too much time writing post-its, changing status of tasks manually, blocking tasks and making recurring tasks by hand every day or every week;

» have the ability to communicate with our developers and sales team via the online platform by linking related cards on our board with cards on their Kanban boards.

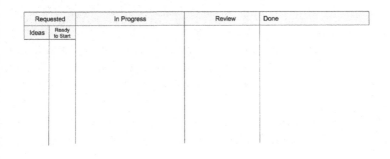

One of the problems that was specific to our marketing team was that we had only one designer available to us. He was the obvious bottleneck, constantly receiving work requests, sometimes only as a verbal 'could you also do this…'. Our team established a pull mechanism (another principle of Lean) in which Kanban cards for every task assigned to the designer were created in the 'Requested' section of the board and prioritized based on the marketing team deadlines. From that moment on, the designer was responsible to pull work, one card at a time, when he had the bandwidth to take it on. When the design card was moved to the 'Done' column, the team could add the designs to the various ongoing campaigns.

As we got used to working on our Kanban board, we became even more specific about the stages of our process. By the six-month mark, our board had a much more detailed structure from which we could collect valuable data about the way we worked:

Ideas were a glorified backlog with the top contenders for our next tasks, but did not contain anything urgent.

Ready to Start was a column reserved for tasks that directly contributed to one or more of the marketing campaigns at hand in that particular period.

Follow Up would keep the cards that were brought back from the 'Review' section and needed to be refined in order to move to 'Done'. These were often higher priority and would be addressed first thing before the others.

In Progress would host cards that were currently being worked on.

Waiting on Relative would keep clusters of cards that were linked to each other with a relative relationship and were waiting for one or more of their relatives to reach this stage in order to move to 'Done' as a cluster.

Waiting for Review is a queue column for cards that are waiting for a review from the team lead.

Review in Progress is an activity column in which cards are actively being reviewed by the team lead.

Review Complete is a queue column in which cards have been reviewed and pending implementation to be moved to the final step of their completion.

Tracking Others would keep cards, the progress of which relies on a third party's actions.

Experiment in Progress hosts cards that represent experiments we are actively tracking or have been running for several weeks, in order to keep them at bay. These tend to be reviewed every week or every couple of days depending on the overall duration of the activity.

After our team read David J. Anderson's *Kanban: Successful Evolutionary Change for Your Technology Business* through the prism of our marketing backgrounds, we added the work-in-progress limits to our board. Each of our team members could have a maximum of two endeavours in progress at once. Since our initial Kanban set-up, our WIP limits have become even stricter, with one task in progress per person for a single board. In the traditional marketing game, multitasking is often commended. However, we decided to try the Kanban approach and optimize for efficiency, not for juggling. This, of course, was met with some discomfort on the side of the team, but with the mutual consensus that this was the best strategy for the team, the adaptation process to the new WIP limits was felt positively among the team members. Even though it took a lot of discipline to apply WIP limits, we saw less multitasking and, consequently, more work getting completed as opposed to abandoned. Essentially, this eliminated the inventory of half-completed articles, pending campaigns and collaborations I anticipated would accrue (as it had in the past during other projects I've worked on). In our humble marketing powerhouse, if you started something, you had to see it through, save for exceptional circumstances. We implemented specific features of the digital Kanban platform we were using in order to structure our process into a predictable and reliable workflow of consistently valuable campaigns.

Business Rules within the system were set up in order to auto-create recurring task cards in the 'Requested' column of our board based on need. These rules also sent email notifications to the team members if the WIP limits were exceeded. Furthermore, another business rule would automatically archive tasks from the 'Done' column after they had spent one month there.

Analytics were used with a three-fold purpose: to monitor the Cumulative Flow diagram in order to identify bottlenecks; to keep an eye out for cards with an abnormally high cycle time; and to resolve them to keep them progressing, monitoring task distribution by each assignee and type of task passing through the workflow.

Setting up **card relationships in a hierarchy** was a helpful mapping feature of digital Kanban boards that would have been near to impossible on a physical board (I've seen people show relationships using strings between post-its). For us, it was essential to be able to show the way individual task cards relate to each other and how they relate to larger portfolio parent cards, which we referred to as campaign cards.

As a subcategory of the available card relationships, **predecessor & successor** is the one we used the most. It allowed us to enforce the order in which cards needed to be completed. In other words, if the defined predecessor card was not in the 'Done' column, then the successor card could not move from the 'Requested' to the 'In Progress' section.

On our main dashboard, **measuring process efficiency** became a way of tracking the work patterns of the team as a whole. Efficiency measured the ratio between how long our task cards spent in the queue columns, waiting for someone to allow them to continue on in the process, versus how long our cards spent in activity columns, being actively worked on by a member of the team.

Creating flexible, practical solutions to common marketing problems

Communication problems faced by marketing teams exist on several levels: internally among the members of the team, interdepartmentally within the organization, as well as externally with the targeted value network. From the very beginning, we were struggling with internal and interdepartmental communication. Between our team members, we implemented the Agile practice of daily stand-up meetings so that we could share goals, achievements and struggles on a day-to-day basis. We met at an odd time (10:08a.m.) each morning, lateness was not tolerated, and we remained standing for the duration of the meeting to make sure it wouldn't drag.

The division between sales and marketing represented our interdepartmental communication woes. It meant that any communication with a trialling or paying customer was followed by a trip to the sales department to find out whether anything of note was pending or had transpired previously with that customer, in terms of upsells, feature requests, and any feedback that might have been collected. We found a way to combat this by creating linkages between cards that were related to customers who already existed in the sales, customer-support or customer-success boards. Each customer represented a portfolio parent card that could contain its history as the group of its other relative cards. This allowed us to form clusters of action items about an organization or a person, such as a map of our relationship with them.

Kanban also aided our campaign management. Apart from cross-board, task cards that were affiliated with a particular campaign were linked between each other right on the marketing board using relationships such as parent, child, relative and predecessor/successor. This was particularly helpful during the breakdown process of a campaign idea. We decided that a conceptual course of action was not actionable until it was broken down into assigned tasks with concrete deadlines. As the head of marketing, this was helpful to me because I could monitor the tasks associated with a single campaign (as child cards) by tracking the parent cards (to which all affiliate child cards were linked) and monitoring the progress of its relatives.

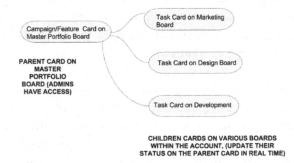

In the Kanban Portfolio Management scenario, the CEO or Project Manager is likely looking at a Portfolio Board that is linked to all the new additions or campaigns that are being worked on in various boards throughout the account, in other words, in various other teams. The Master Board will look something like this:

Next 6 Mnt	Next 3 Mnt	Breakdown	Breakdown Done	In Progress					Done
				Ready for Dev	Tech Analysis	In Development	Ready for Sign-off	Ready for Production	
Reporting and Analytics									

A single card on the Portfolio board can be linked to various cards on other boards such as Development, Design, Quality as well as Marketing.

Campaign/Feature Card on Master Portfolio Board

Task Card on Marketing Board

Task Card on Design Board

Task Card on Development

PARENT CARD ON MASTER PORTFOLIO BOARD (ADMINS HAVE ACCESS)

CHILDREN CARDS ON VARIOUS BOARDS WITHIN THE ACCOUNT, (UPDATE THEIR STATUS ON THE PARENT CARD IN REAL TIME)

Marketing teams (and we were no exception) are typically made up of members from varying professional backgrounds and must work at becoming experts in different areas of marketing for specific campaigns they undertake. We tackled this problem of lack of specific experience by integrating Kanban cards related to specific research, webinar or professional literature so that these could be executed to completion as one would run a campaign. We referred to this as our education campaign. This mindset allowed us to target areas of improvement like SEO, link-building, content marketing and PR and learn more about each of them. In the beginning, training cards were made to share knowledge through internal presentations among the members of the team and later on external trainers were brought in to elevate the knowledge level of the group. This helped the team to pursue the Lean principle of perfection, not only on a day-to-day basis in our communal activities but also as a personal goal.

In addition, having everything tracked and stored within the searchable Kanban platform meant that we were able to recall elements of campaigns that were being tracked in the system and all of it was available at a glance, whenever we needed it. The clusters of Kanban cards, as well as the Kanban board generally, became knowledge radiators for all the projects that the team had pursued up until this point and could be shared easily with new team members who needed to catch up.

Depending on the campaign, the success of marketing activities can be difficult to measure. Performance metrics of the team are rarely tracked while KPIs for campaigns often get reviewed or reported only as a retrospective once the campaign is over. The lack of reporting problems is one of the most threatening to marketers and is often a result of the very nature of the professionals who tend to work in this field. Typically, marketers tend to be creatives who struggle with taking an analytical approach to their artistic pursuits. In truth, marketing is a combination of art and data. One without the other will not produce the desired result. Luckily, Kanban encourages measurable goals upon which the team can improve over time. The analytics arsenal linked to our digital Kanban board allowed us to collect reports about our own team's efficiency as well as measure the success of our campaigns based on KPIs we were tracking within our Kanban cards. For example, successful versus unsuccessful link-building pursuits were measured using custom fields in our Kanban cards. We used our digital tool to generate pie graphs to visualize success rate on a weekly basis; we currently have a success rate of 20% of successful pursuits, which includes pitches, responding to journalists' queries and writing to connect with media editors. We have been monitoring this metric and experimenting with ways of improving it.

In monitoring our block resolution time, we noticed a 50% decrease of the time it used to take our team to address blocked cards and resolve them so that they could move forward through the process. It meant that we were dealing with blockages faster and not letting a card just idle in the flow. We began monitoring our process efficiency as the ratio between how long our materials and content cards spent waiting for review versus how long we actually spent actively working on them through a dashboard widget. We have tracked that our efficiency has grown from 20% to 60% since the initiation of our digital Kanban board. However, what seems to be most important is that, in tracking these metrics in general, the Lean principle of continuous improvement has become entrenched in the way we decide what we will work on, how we will approach it, and how we will measure it. To prevent bottlenecks in the process, we kept track of how many tasks were in each phase of the process using the Cumulative Flow diagram, typical to Kanban. This chart gave us a sense of the tasks we were accumulating and the trends we could expect down the line.

All Lean and all marketing processes are flow-based (or, at least, they should be). If you're working in iterations, then you might be taking a risk with your time and budget resources. Imagine a company that provides a paid service that you love. One day, you stop receiving their regular newsletter, their social media accounts go silent, their website hasn't been updated in months, and they no longer participate in industry events. In terms of marketing, predictable delivery of high-quality campaigns that make sense is just as important as basing them on creative ideas. In Lean, this is referred to as the value stream towards your customer. A Lean team's goal is to make the stream of value towards the customer as consistent as possible in order to build trust, loyalty, and their own reliability. Blowing the budget on a single campaign is not an option when you are aiming to build a sustainable marketing strategy consistently attracting new customers to your product.

Our team focused on marketing hacks that would build upon each other and continue to bring returns (measured as number of new trials, increased traffic to our website, SEO benchmarks or even accumulated data from experiments), even after we had shifted focus to a different campaign. For example, we opted for building high-quality content, link-building with industry influencers and landing page conversion experiments instead of social media, television ads, billboards and the like. As Lean marketers, we found ways to measure each of our endeavours and allocated a more significant bulk of the budget only towards campaigns that showed promise during the experimentation phase (a stage in our workflow, as shown on our Kanban board).

We aimed to create a flow of marketing efforts that would make us more visible to our existing customers as well as potential users of our platform. Each campaign complemented its preceding and following campaigns in building a stable stream of content towards our target audience instead of an expensive blitz.

After working on our digital Kanban board and Lean principles for between six and twelve months, we observed the following benefits:

> » No more 'he said, she said', just data right on the board, accessible from anywhere with an Internet connection. This minimized the need for constant reporting and prevented information loss.

> » Remote team members became more included in the work process and, consequently, took on more initiative and responsibility.

> » Knowledge-sharing and the tracking of information in a communal database (the board itself) for the sake of continuous improvement were encouraged.

> » Team began to focus on improving the metrics of their own process in addition to campaign KPIs. Metrics such as card cycle time and overall efficiency of processes became important to the team.

> » With a clear process for testing, research and education, the team became more eager to test something before jumping into things haphazardly.

> » Automation got rid of a lot of the manual aspects of managing recurring tasks, WIP limits and assigning recurring tasks.

» We developed a more predictable and stable flow in the way we dealt with requested tasks and entire campaign breakdowns. We became one of the most consistent teams in the company.

» The team began to base more of their suggestions on what would bring value to our customers and identify new ones rather than just any other 'cool' ideas.

Couldn't we have run a similar marketing operation without adopting Lean and Kanban as a method of application?

There are probably examples of marketing operations that managed to run smoothly and exceed their goals without applying the Lean methodology and, more particularly, the Kanban method. Similarly, there are a lot of very successful start-ups that began in someone's garage making use of scrap equipment to validate their product. However, modern organizations have the advantage of functioning effectively and efficiently by making use of tried and tested approaches such as Lean and Agile, which are aimed at optimizing resources. This could potentially eliminate a lot of trial and error that other organizations have gone through to validate that these principles have certain benefits if implemented correctly throughout a team. The Lean Kanban workflow management approach has helped companies in the manufacturing and product development industries aim higher and deliver projects with greater speed and quality. The field of Marketing can also benefit from this type of thinking and structure in order to grow in a fast and stable way as an industry.

Lean Marketing managed to bring positive results to our SaaS marketing team as well as to our organization on a broader level. Furthermore, it ended up bringing our team and product closer to our customers because they knew they could count on us to consistently deliver high-quality results. Many of our customers stick with us because they appreciate the Lean values we represent and the way we have applied them to build the product they also use. After overcoming the typical marketing challenges of lack of communication, budget, reporting and experience by using Lean best practices, we used Kanban to ensure that our team has an opportunity to define new, greater challenges and evolve towards perfection.

Over the course of the development of our Lean Kanban marketing team up until this point, our team's efficiency has increased threefold; our tool has transformed into a feature-rich platform; our organization has tripled in size; and we have begun to expand to new markets. Needless to say, we believe in the power of Lean and recommend a Lean Kanban implementation to any marketing team out there.

Case Study Eight: Agile Marketing at Audodesk

Contributed by Peter Billante, Software Products Leader | VP Product Management | Marketing

When we first started our Agile Marketing program with a Scrum process, at the end of the two-week sprint cycles, we could see that nothing was getting done or things would be only partly done. No one had tracked the work in progress, and I realized this process was not working. We had a cross-functional team of individuals each reporting to other managers setting their priorities. It was not a good fit for the Scrum process and we had to shut it down. Scrum was not working for this team, and it didn't help produce good results.

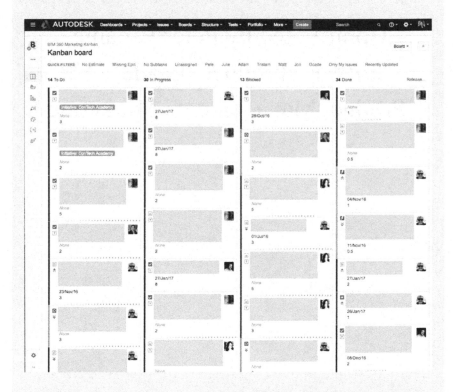

Following this, we spent some time thinking about a specific goal we wanted the marketing team to achieve and what we needed for this particular customer; the customer in this case was the product line that we were trying to market. As a large company, we were dealing with hundreds of products and our marketing thus far had felt as if we were part of that list of products, but somewhat distant from the market we wanted to serve. We had very good brand marketing, high-level messaging and thought-leading content at a company level. To connect with the right target customers, we decided that this product line needed an inbound marketing approach. However, we didn't have one specific place for customers to find out about our products; we didn't offer a great experience for someone who wanted to learn about it, to see who it was for, and what problems our products solve. Thus, we developed a strategy to create an inbound marketing program and the kind of team and skills that we needed to run it. We hired and built the initial core team of eight people. We relaunched our Agile Marketing program with that team, a dedicated unit of people whose only focus was the inbound marketing program for the marketing of a specific product within a larger range. Fast-forwarding to the end of the story, this marketing program was a great success in its first iteration and continues to be very successful today.

My biggest learning so far, and I validated this with other people in the agile marketing Meetup groups, is that you must have a dedicated team that buys into the process and stays committed to it. They should understand the goals they are shooting for, but also understand agile as a process for achieving their goals. Highly matrixed teams that report to different managers all have different goals and priorities, so we could not always count on them to get things done towards marketing our specific product. Having a dedicated team was the first step in the right direction. The second step was to figure out what the right process was. My other learning from this first iteration of Scrum was that marketing is not like a product team where the team is focused on shipping a product release to the customer. A product release is a clear deliverable: everyone on the team knows what they are working towards and it's always a team effort.

In marketing, however, things don't necessarily work the same way. I have talked to leaders in different agile organizations and the closest comparable situation seems to be where you may have teams that are only doing website development and their aim is to ship web updates. Many times we have ongoing campaigns that we are iterating on. We launch them, get some data back, and then we iterate again and again. Therefore, there is no single release shipped at the end of sprints, and many times the iterations do not involve the whole team. For example, you may have one or two people who manage paid social media and search advertising campaigns that can often work independently. This is unlike a product release where typically everyone works on the same deliverables, but in different functional roles (development, UX, QA, etc.).

Individuals within agile marketing teams do need to synchronize with each other to coordinate their work and minimize the occurrence of mistakes but, unlike product development, for the most part, they can independently ship (execute campaigns) at any time. The content team can independently ship a blog post mid-sprint and they should be working with the social media lead to do some amplification and generating traffic to that blog. So, I looked at that workflow and decided that I didn't want to force everybody into a process where they feel they have to complete each task within a two-week sprint cycle, because that could feel like an artificial deadline. The risk you take on with artificial deadlines is that people don't always buy into that idea. They might go along with it in the beginning, but they may not be fully committed to the process unless they can see the benefit to themselves or the team. I didn't want to force people into a process. I also had a team of expert marketing professionals, not software developers. They had never done an agile process before and I didn't want to jump in with a heavy process of daily stand-ups, sprint planning meetings, retrospectives and backlog grooming. It felt as if it was just too much to take on at the start, so we decided to start the agile marketing journey in a somewhat lightweight way.

We started with a Kanban-style process. We said that all we are going to do as a team is track and report on three key things: work that is 'To-Do', 'In-Progress', and 'Done'. We scoped these lists for a two-week period, rank-ordered all the cards/tasks, and then all we had to do is manage a three-column Kanban board moving things through the process so we can visualize where we are.

Every day, each person did a check-in, where they would say what they are working on and update the Kanban board. They also said what they have completed and whether there was anything obstructing them from proceeding with what they were currently working on. We also decided to use several tools to support the process because we had a geographically distributed team. Initially, we used Trello, but we quickly realized that we needed something more scalable for filtering and measurement, so we migrated to Jira. Tools such as Trello are very useful for small teams and a good way to start the agile journey. For our daily check-ins, we used Slack to keep the process light, rather than have everybody meet at a specific time, because we were operating in different time zones.

We continued to iterate in two-week cycles within Kanban, looking at what had been done during the previous two weeks and re-prioritizing for the next two weeks. We also started to do retrospectives to find out what worked and what didn't. Then we introduced another stage to our process by creating another board for grooming our backlogs to accommodate ideas from every member of the team and external requests from other teams. And we continuously groomed these backlogs for future cycles.

Next, we started measuring our agile marketing process to find out how well it was working. We wanted to know more about how things were getting done and how long they were taking. We started by looking at the tasks on the Kanban board and counting them. How many tasks were we typically completing every two weeks? We started counting all the 'Done' tasks and realized that because tasks were of different sizes, just counting them as equal wasn't truly representing what we had delivered. We added story-point estimating to our process, and now we can summarize each cycle based on the number of completed story points to measure the process. Now that we've iterated on our agile process over many cycles, we're planning to move to a more standard Scrum-based process again, to help with measurements in the sprints such as burn-down reporting, although we will be implementing Scrum with some modifications for marketing projects.

Case Study Nine: Agile Sales

Contributed by Marina Simonova,
Agile Sales Coach

About me

My name is Marina Simonova and I have been working in sales in Russia's top finance companies for over 10 years. I have extensive experience of implementing Agile in sales and marketing teams in Russia and other European countries. I am glad to share with you my experience and I hope that reading this case study will motivate you to adopt the Agile mindset and methods in your sales and marketing departments – and perhaps even in your whole company. In my opinion, an Agile transformation is the best thing that can happen to any sales or marketing department. However, it will require patience, hard work and the willingness to accept serious changes.

Implementing Agile

Most probably you have already heard of Agile, but perhaps you are not completely familiar with how it works in sales or marketing? The core of agile in this sphere is about changing the quality of interaction, firstly with the client, but also among the employees within the company.

Implementing Agile is not easy; it is not a quick fix, but a journey that starts and unfolds slowly. It requires changing the habits, ways of thinking, and patterns of behaviour of your employees. In 90% of the cases you are likely to see little to no improvement in the first three months. In fact, the opposite is often true. Be prepared that 20–30% of employees, those who are not willing to change, will leave the company. Agile transformation is also particularly important with the leadership of the organization - agile will not work unless the top management also adjusts their values and work patterns. Listed below are some steps for adopting Agile into sales teams.

In order to succeed in your Agile transformation, it is necessary to find and hire a very good Agile coach, but this should be somebody who speaks the language of marketing and sales. This is not just a whim -

here is why:

> » Sales people are very different from IT people. We (sales people) are used to following transcripts (the lines every salesperson has to say during their client call), we are used to following orders from top managers without questioning them. Thus, independent thinking is often eliminated in the sales process. We report the number of cold calls we make and meetings we have, and there is never an opportunity to use our imagination and create anything new. We don't have teams – we are rugged individualists.

> » Marketing is often guilty of working in its own bubble without including sales teams in their campaign planning and execution. What can we do better? Invite sales teams to planning meetings? How about sales teams inviting marketing to client meetings and presentations, so marketing can really understand the world of sales? We don't see salespeople and us as one, we never tried to achieve a common goal! Yes, we are creative, yet we don't always come up with useful products that add value to our clients. Our marketing events are planned a year ahead. The email budget was approved, so we must send emails despite the fact that Instagram has just come onto the market and is so much more convenient. Does this sound familiar?

Both marketing and sales have to change as fast as the world around us is changing. Agile is all about changing the way you think. It's not enough to read a couple of dozen books about Agile, or the Scrum Guide. You need a professional (a good team coach, a facilitator and a mediator) who loves sales and marketing and knows everything about Agile transformations, Kanban and Scrum. This coach will take the team through the hardest times and not let them throw in the towel.

Why I can't recommend taking an Agile transformation on your own

Imagine you are a professional athlete, but after an injury you have gained extra weight. The World Cup is coming soon and you need to get back into shape to compete. What would be more effective? Doing exercises on your own, or having a knowledgeable coach take you to that goal and not letting you aggravate the injury? Agile has been so successful in IT because IT teams hire Agile coaches to help them with the Agile transformation - this is the best way of successfully adopting Agile. Good Agile coaches aren't cheap, so it is important that during their time with the company the coach trains in-house Agile coaches who can take over the Agile transformation when the external coach has to leave. Normally, with each company, the coach works on site once or twice a week for 6 to 18 months and in that time they train between two and six in-house Agile coaches. The Agile coach pays serious attention to training Scrum Masters, as they are the main drivers of whichever approach a company takes: Agile, Scrum or Kanban. Once you have a great Agile coach, the next step is to simply select the people for the pilot team and launch the Agile transformation.

Selecting a team

How do you choose the people for the pilot team?

Get all the company employees together (if it's a large company, get the sales and marketing departments together). Give a brief introduction about Agile and then let the company owner explain to everyone the reasons why coaches have been invited and the purpose for the Agile transformation. The pilot team is then chosen. There are three options of doing this:

Volunteers: Have a meeting with all the salespeople or all the marketing consultants, tell them about Agile and ask for volunteers for the pilot project. 'Who has the most courage?' All those willing to be on the team raise their hands and form the first pilot team.

The 'No Choice' option: The company management simply selects a department by informing them: 'Starting next Monday you are going

Agile!' It's very important that the company leadership explains to the department why it was them who were chosen, and informs the employees of other departments that this particular department will comprise the pilot team.

Losers: This option is my favourite! You take the worst performing sales team that continuously misses its sales targets and tell them: 'You have a chance to change everything!' This option has two advantages: a) the whole company will be watching this pilot project with great interest; and b) the team will really want to prove to everyone that they can be the best. Trust me, they will.

After the team members have been chosen, you proceed with a three-day training period. It is advisable to hold the training in a separate building so that for the whole three days the employees can be immersed in Agile, rather than return to their workplaces and be distracted by their daily work.

Training

A strong start is very important!

To implement the three-day training, you will need a professional Agile coach. For the training, use games and Agile simulations to acquaint the team with Agile values, Scrum and Kanban frameworks. Foster teamwork. This training period is the perfect time to define the roles within the team and choose the Scrum Master. The product owner (the Sales or Marketing Director) has to participate in the training. During the first two days the team learns to be an Agile team, work together, and create its own team values. Devote the third day to planning. Create a three-month backlog: a precise list of what the team is expected to achieve over the next three months. A strong launch of the team is critical. Therefore, hire a good Agile coach who will not only run the training, but also monitor the team for these first three months. In Agile transformations for sales and marketing I often use Scrum with all its roles and events (the changes it offers are more radical than those in Kanban). If I do use Kanban, I always include Scrum roles (Product Owner, Scrum Master) together with all the events as described in the Scrum Guide.

Roles

Definitely go with the roles. There are three: the team, the Scrum Master, and the Product Owner.

1.   A department is now a team.

2.   The Head of department is now a Scrum Master.

3.   The Sales/Marketing Director is now a Product Owner.

Let's explain these one at a time (but in a different order).

> The role of **Scrum Master** is a very important one, this is a new generation leader: a servant leader. The Scrum Master does not tell the team what it should do, does not assign tasks and, I will go so far as to say, does not fire people. The team does that. The job of the Scrum Master is to help the team reach its goals, to coach the team, to facilitate events, to inspire the team and believe in it, to help team members solve conflicts, and to remove any obstacles from the team's way. The Scrum Master motivates people to achieve great results and continually improve the quality of work of each team member; they handle issues in relations with other departments and communicate with the Product Owner to protect the team from any pressure that might come from that person.

The skill set of a Scrum Master includes leadership, coaching, facilitation and mediation

> The **Product Owner** has the authority to make decisions. Usually this is a Sales Director or a Marketing Director. The

Product Owner has strategic vision which they share with the team. It's up to the team to decide how to implement this vision. The Product Owner must be available for the team: they should always be present at planning sessions, demos, and, if invited by the team, at retrospectives. To use a metaphor, the Product Owner is the ship's captain who shows the way to the hidden treasure, whereas the team is the crew who decide how to sail and how to avoid a shipwreck. The captain is responsible for pointing the team to the island where the treasure is hidden. They are responsible for the end result!

The Product Owner must have the authority to make decisions, have a clear understanding of the sales strategy or the marketing strategy, and possess strong leadership skills. This is a highly qualified professional.

» The third role is **the team** itself. For many years Sales Managers have worked independently. Each one divided the clients into his own clients, and those of other managers, even though the company 'owned' all the clients. I've often noticed that when a Sales Manager is on vacation, their clients get very little attention. The deputising Sales Manager is unwilling to work with 'other managers' clients'. I have always resisted this attitude! The world has changed and so have the clients. We all (the employees) represent one company and all its clients are OUR clients. Are you familiar with the tough competition in the sales department? Everyone follows a clear plan of action. There is a prescribed script, call targets and 'personal meeting' targets for each sales manager, and so on. However, the times have changed and the sales algorithm is not the same any longer. Clients know everything they need about the product from the Internet. We need to put our heads together and create added value for the clients, so that they will buy from us. And for that we need to be a team, and not just a sales team, but one team - together with the marketing managers. If the company is not large, create cross-functional teams, combine both marketing managers with sales and pre-sales managers. In large companies, form an Agile sales team (between seven and nine people) and an Agile marketing team. They should continually interact and attend each other's Agile meetings and team demos. Once a month there will be a retrospective for all sales and marketing managers. In the office, the team members should be seated together (it's not a distributed team). Marketing managers should sit next to sales managers. The IT department should be sitting close by, because you cannot sell without IT technologies these days.

Create new roles and put the people together. Do everything possible to enable sales, marketing and IT managers to continually interact!

Let the team have a taste of Agile

OK, so you have the team, you've done the training, and selected the Scrum Master and the Product Owner. You've created the backlog and done the planning. What now? My suggestion is to do Sprint Zero with the team. A sprint is a period of time during which the sales or marketing team sets goals, reaches them, demonstrates their results and works on improving their performance. Sprints can last for anything between one and four weeks.

For the first three months, I advise the team to have one-week sprints. Have Sprint Zero for the team to adapt to the changes. The backlog of Sprint Zero contains such tasks as planning the seating space for the team, putting up the boards, purchasing sticky notes, and so on. During Sprint Zero there is a demo and a retrospective. Since this is a training sprint, there is no need to invite the company leaders to the demo of Sprint Zero. Have the team, the Scrum Master, the Product Owner, and certainly the Agile coach (who will mentor the team for the next three months) attend this demo. Don't take on complicated tasks during Sprint Zero - let the team adapt to the changes.

Now I would like to go into more detail about Scrum events, which I, as a coach, always attend and facilitate. The Product Owner and the Scrum Master receive feedback from me there.

The scrum board and daily stand-up meetings

Let's create a Scrum board.

For the first six months I recommend having a physical (not electronic) board with sticky notes. Divide the space on the board into four columns:

> » Column 1: TO DO – comprises all that needs to be done during the week (in a one-week sprint). Place the notes with undone tasks here.

> » Column 2: DOING – when the team starts working on a task, move the note with that task here from TO DO.

> » Column 3: DONE – move the note here when the task is complete.

> » Column 4: 'APPROVED' – issues, approvals, etc. should be listed here. Move the note here if the task isn't being solved and the solution depends on external circumstances.

Every team member uses their own colour of sticky notes or signs their name on their notes. An avatar picture or a miniature photo can be used to personalize notes. The point is: it must be clear to anyone who takes a look at the Scrum board whose task is where.

The daily stand-up meeting

This daily event runs for less than 15 minutes and takes place at the same time every day. As the team (including the Scrum Master) answers three questions, the sticky notes are moved to the appropriate columns:

> » What did I do yesterday to accomplish my sprint goals?

» What will I be doing today to accomplish my sprint goals?

» Do I need anyone's assistance?

Use a physical board with sticky notes for six months (but please note that this will not work for off-site teams). My experience tells me that it may take the team one month to begin appreciating the scrum board or the Kanban board.

Events – the planning and the backlog

Planning is a crucial event for the Agile team. It takes two hours for every one-week sprint; four hours for a two-week sprint; and so on. The team, the Scrum Master, and the Product Owner must all participate.

The backlog for sales and marketing is a list of all the tasks that need to be accomplished by the team during a certain period of time. For sales, the period is one quarter. For marketing, it depends on the tasks they have, but definitely not less than a month. The backlog includes both quantitative indicators (the sales targets, the number of website visitors, the number of buyers, etc.) and qualitative indicators (improvement of business processes, creating a new product or service for the client). All backlog tasks must follow the SMART model.

A sprint backlog is a list of all tasks that the team undertakes during one sprint. It is crucial to set the main goal for each sprint. It must be based on the tasks the team will be working on. By the end of the sprint, the goal must be achieved!

Planning is an event during which the product owner tells the team WHICH TASKS from the backlog need to be done during this sprint. The team plans HOW they will accomplish these tasks. Traditionally, in sales and marketing, top managers instruct employees as to how to do their job, and then monitor their every step. Agile boasts having self-organized teams. Their members generate ideas, have brainstorming sessions, and plan their working day on their own. The product owner does not control the day-to-day activities of the team. All the tasks are set during the planning session.

It's important for the team to plan its work for the following sprint. The Scrum Master facilitates this event and makes sure that the product owner does not use their authority to put pressure on the team or force the team to take on more tasks than can be accomplished. The Scrum Master also makes sure that all team members clearly understand everything in the backlog. For the first three to six months, the team will really benefit from the support of a professional Agile coach as it is necessary that the team, the Scrum Master and the Product Owner develop completely new patterns of behaviour.

Events – the demo and the retrospective

A demo is the demonstration of the achieved results which takes one hour (in a one-week sprint). Anyone can take part. During the demo the team explains which tasks it had to accomplish, and which results it was able to achieve. Any issues in collaborating with other departments are made known at the demo so that a common solution may be worked out. I recommend ensuring that the top management of the company is present at the demo, especially when the company is running a pilot project. It is very important for the success of the Agile transformation of the whole company that the company owner or the general director is present at this event. I include the following clause in my contract with the company: 'The company owner or the general director must be present at the demos during the first three months'.

A retrospective is an event that takes place at the end of each sprint after the demo; in a one-week sprint it normally takes one hour. Here, the team works on the continual improvement of its performance. I believe this to be the engine that drives the team. The team answers two questions: 'How did the sprint go?' and 'What can we do better in the next sprint?' The team may wish to invite the Product Owner to take part in the retrospective.

During the retrospective the team deals with conflicts and openly discusses anything that was an obstacle to their work. The team also remembers to praise its individual members for their victories! It is vital to recognize your victories in order to exceed your targets. The support of a professional coach is needed for the first two to six months as this event is the most difficult one to get right and the most important one for the team.

Anyone can come to the demo. Post invitations all over the office and put them on the top managers' calendars. A retrospective is a very personal event for the team. It helps the team to improve itself and create a backlog (list) of improvements to be implemented during the next sprint.

Main issues related to an Agile transformation

I have made all my recommendations (above) bearing in mind that the Agile team uses the Scrum or Kanban framework. The core values of Scrum are responsibility, courage, focus, transparency and respect. It takes time for these values to be adopted by the Agile team. Let me also warn you that some people will not be willing to change. You must be prepared to see 20–30% of the employees leave the company.

The top-five difficulties you may face on your journey to an Agile transformation can be summarized as follows:

1.   Don't expect any major results from the team during the first three months. The team needs this time to learn to work together and to accept Agile and Scrum values.

2.   Absence of trust and the constant pressure the Product Owner puts on the team are the two most frequent difficulties you will

come up against during the Agile transformation. These two elements will demotivate the team and decrease output, so they need to be managed.

3.   Sales managers find it very difficult to take on responsibility. At first, people will try to shift blame onto the Scrum Master or each other.

4.   Looking for the guilty party and pointing out mistakes of the other team members are ancient habits that can be very difficult to resist. Look for solutions and opportunities, don't dwell on the past.

5.   The top management may not be ready to make changes. Middle and top managers will have to undergo the greatest changes,as they are used to having authority and making decisions on their own. Therefore, it is difficult for them to adapt to the new Agile culture.

To change the corporate culture even in one (relatively small) team is very difficult. Be patient and after six or seven months you will witness your targets doubled – or even trebled! Your marketing teams will create unique and customer-oriented products, which will lead to a significant increase in the profitability of the whole company. However, all of this will only happen if the top management undergoes the changes alongside the rest of the employees.

Perhaps I might have scared you with my account of the difficulties involved in Agile transformations in sales and marketing. I have – more than once – intentionally stressed that any changes in thinking patterns, habits and actions take time and require courage, discipline and hard work. The Agile coach will help you make it through the most difficult period of the first three to six months. Then, between six and twelve months after the launch (perhaps just eight months after the launch) of the Agile transformation, you will be rewarded with an Agile sales or marketing team that will easily exceed its targets by anything between two and six times. This team will also create the kinds of product that clients will line up for, and for which they will give your company the highest praise. And what is most important – you and your co-workers will be happy at work, totally involved and giving it your best. That is the prize that makes undergoing the hard Agile transformation course worthwhile. Trust me, I have witnessed successful Agile sales teams that tripled their sales targets!

I sincerely wish you a successful Agile transformation in your sales and marketing departments!

If you have any questions, you can find me on LinkedIn

References and Bibliography

Adkins, L. (2010) *Coaching agile teams: a companion for ScrumMasters, agile coaches, and project managers in transition*; Boston, MA: Pearson Education Inc.

Anderson, D.J. (2010) *Kanban: Successful Evolutionary Change for Your Technology Business,* Sequim, WA: Blue Hole Press

Bock, L. (2015) *Work Rules! Insights from inside Google that will transform how you live and lead*; London: John Murray (Publishers)

Boeg, J. (2012) *Priming Kanban: A 10 step guide to optimizing flow in your software delivery system, 2nd Edition*; Aarhus, Denmark: Trifork A/S

Bradberry, T. and Greaves, J. (2009) *Emotional Intelligence 2.0*; San Diego, CA: TalentSmart

Cohn, M. (2006) *Agile Estimating and Planning; Upper Saddle River,* NJ: Pearson Education, Inc.

Derby, E. & Larsen, D. (2006) *Agile Retrospectives: Making Good Teams Great;*Raleigh, NC: The Pragmatic Programmers, LLC

Goulston, M. (2010) *Just Listen;*New York, NY: AMACOM

Magretta, J. (2012) *Understanding Michael Porter: The Essential Guide to Competition and Strategy;* Boston, MA: Harvard Business School Publishing

Patterson, K., Grenny, J., McMillan, R. and Switzler, A. (2012) *Crucial Conversations: Tools for Talking When Stakes Are High*; New

York, NY: McGraw Hill

Peppers, D. (2016) *Customer Experience: What, How and Why Now*; TeleTech

Pink, D. H. (2009) Drive: *The Surprising Truth About What Motivates Us*; New York, NY: Riverhead Books

Portigal, S. (2013) *Interviewing Users: How To Uncover Compelling Insights*; Brooklyn, NY: Rosenfeld Media, LLC

Ries, E. (2011)The Lean Startup: How Constant Innovation Creates Radically Successful Businesses;UK: Portfolio Penguin

Rosenberg, M.B. (2015) *Non-Violent Communication, 3rd Edition;* Encinitas, CA: PuddleDancer Press

Rubin, K.S. (2013) *Essential Scrum: a practical guide to the most popular agile process;* Ann Arbor, Michigan: Pearson Education Inc.

Sharp, D. (1987) *Personality Types: Jung's Model of Typology*; Toronto, Canada: Inner City Books

Stellman, A. & Greene, J. (2015) *Learning Agile*; Sebastopol, CA: O'Reilly Media, Inc.

Sutherland, J. (2014) Scrum: *The Art of Doing Twice the Work in Half the Time*; London: Random House Business Books

Tan, C-M. (2012) Search Inside Yourself: *The Unexpected Path to Achieving Success, Happiness (and World Peace)*; New York, NY: HarperCollins Publishers

Watts, G. (2013) Scrum Mastery: *From Good To Great Servant Leadership*; Cheltenham, Glos: Inspect & Adapt Ltd.

Niven, P.R. and Lamorte, B. (2016) *Objectives and Key Results*: Driving Focus, Alignment and Engagement with OKRs; Wiley

Corporate F&A

Alessandra, T. and Hunsaker, P.L. (1993) *Communicating at Work*; Simon and Schuster

Author's Biography

Femi has a wealth of experience and certifications in search marketing, customer experience, web analytics, content marketing and Agile marketing. He was part of agile marketing teams in global B2B and B2C companies operating in a wide range of industries, including: IT, software development, pharmaceuticals, telecommunications, retail, marketing, media and non-profits. He has extensive experience of training and mentoring marketing teams towards developing and executing successful integrated marketing strategies. Femi holds an MSc in Marketing from the Heriot-Watt University and is currently working on completing his ICF coaching certifications.

My Agile Beginnings

I first experienced agility in marketing at the young age of 19. I had just started university in my native Nigeria and needed a job to pay my way through school. I found out about the poultry business when I accompaniedmy cousin, a local plumber,to a local poultry farm to fix some broken pipes and immediately decided to start my own small scale poultry business. Due to my lack of experience in this area, I decided to speak to local farmers and conduct my own research about the production process and the requirements for raisingBroiler chickens.

The production and marketing of the Broiler chickens was seasonal in nature and was most heavy in the Easter and Christmas period. I bought my first batch of 150 Broiler chickens at the end January and raised them towards Easter, to be sold at the local market; I then started the next production iteration in early October to be sold during the Christmas and New Year's celebrations. I had little knowledge of business or marketing, apart from what I leant in the first year of My Business Administration course. I did, however, very quickly come to understand the laws of supply and demand and the impact of their interaction on price. I also started recognizing that every business model has two things at the opposite ends of the spectrum: profitability and customer satisfaction. I appreciated that, in order to survive and compete with bigger poultry businesses, I needed to pay more attention to satisfying my customers and I made a conscious decision not to make any profit from my business in the first year: my main goal in this period was to satisfy my customers first and earn their trust.

All this happened in 1998 in Africa, back when most of the world knew little to nothing about mobile phones and even less aboutGoogle analytics or digital marketing as avenues for gathering customer insights and feedback. My only recourse was to observe the behavior and body language of my customersin order to understand exactly what they wanted. Each time I interacted with a customer, I learnt something new about them and this helped me to develop a large customer based that trusted me enough to deposit half of the payment 4 months in advance for the Broiler chickens for their seasonal celebrations – I was their supplier of choice. This business lasted for 3 years and generated enough profit for me to live comfortably throughout my studies. The industries I've worked in since this time are extremely varied and span IT, software development, pharmaceuticals, non-profits, retail and marketing, but the core principles of customer satisfaction I learned in this period of my life are applicable in all of them and are still with me in everything I do. And if you want to be Number 1 in your industry – you should make sure you embed them within your customer's journey too!

Femi Olajiga

Made in the USA
Columbia, SC
15 December 2017